JOINING TOGETHER, STANDING APART:
NATIONAL IDENTITIES AFTER NAFTA

NAFTA Law and Policy Series

VOLUME 4

Series Editors

Seymour J. Rubin, B.A., LL.B., LL.M.

Professor of Law, Emeritus in Residence,
Washington College of Law, American University

Dean C. Alexander, B.A., J.D., LL.M.

Formerly Director, International Business Center,
Grant Thornton, Santiago and
Director, The NAFTA Research Institute,
Washington, D.C.

The book series will include high-quality studies on different aspects of NAFTA, including legal analysis and commentary on the Agreement. Among the numerous areas that will be covered in the series are NAFTA topics as diverse as agriculture, dispute settlement, environment, intellectual property rights, investment, and labor. Contributors will be drawn from the legal profession, business, government, and the academic community. The series is designed to ensure that practitioners, corporate counsel, government officials, academics, and businessmen will gain a thorough understanding of the multi-faceted legal and economic implications of NAFTA.

The titles published in this series are listed at the end of this volume.

Joining Together, Standing Apart: National Identities after NAFTA

edited by

Dorinda G. Dallmeyer

Dean Rusk Center for International and Comparative Law

KLUWER LAW INTERNATIONAL

THE HAGUE / LONDON / BOSTON

A C.I.P. Catalogue record for this book is available from the Library of Congress.

ISBN 90-411-0483-6

Published by Kluwer Law International,
P.O. Box 85889, 2508 CN The Hague, The Netherlands.

Sold and distributed in the U.S.A. and Canada
by Kluwer Law International,
675 Massachusetts Avenue, Cambridge, MA 02139, U.S.A.

In all other countries, sold and distributed
by Kluwer Law International, Distribution Centre,
P.O. Box 322, 3300 AH Dordrecht, The Netherlands.

Printed on acid-free paper

To Louis B. Sohn

TABLE OF CONTENTS

FOREWORD

When I think about the U.S.-Mexico relationship, I am reminded of a comment made by Talleyrand, the great French foreign minister of the Napoleonic era. At a lunch, an aide whispered to him that an eminent rival had died. He responded, "I wonder what he meant by that." So much of U.S.-Mexican relations has focused on trying to find ulterior motives for rather transparent events, of infusing deep-seated fears or lingering hopes into a relationship in which a simpler explanation might suffice and permit a more normal relationship.

I am thinking, in particular, of two rather important events that occurred in the space of two weeks in December 1994. From December 9 to 11, 1994, the Summit of the Americas occurred in Miami. President Clinton hosted 33 leaders from throughout the hemisphere who had been elected, who were civilians, accountable to their people. Elections were not free and fair in the same degree in every country; there were a couple of exceptions, but nonetheless these were civilian-technocrats for the first time in history, approaching inter-Americans relations from the perspective of the same agenda based on integration and trade, democratization and governance, and environmental and development sustainability. It was a significant event which was made possible largely because of an initiative which had come from Mexico several years before that culminated with the North American Free Trade Agreement.

The outcome of the summit was a goal that in ten years, the hemisphere would have a free trade area. It raised people's hopes. But two weeks later, Mexico -- the very country that had given rise to the initiative that had culminated with this Summit of the Americas -- was faced with a crisis that shook the entire region. The government devalued the peso, by 15 percent, but the peso then began to plummet so quickly that it called into question the North American Free Trade Agreement that had begun barely one year ago, and it resurrected all the old stereotypes of Mexico.

Those are two very interesting metaphors, if you will, of our relationship. At the summit, Latin America, led by the United States, had walked to the steps of

vii

the first world, and most people thought Latin America had arrived. Yet two weeks later, the collapse of the peso led everybody to ask, "Has Latin America gone around the bend?" The question I would like to address relates to NAFTA. Specifically, was the North American Free Trade Agreement a success or a failure? Was there something we hadn't anticipated adequately when the agreement was negotiated?

First, let's start with definition. What is the North American Free Trade Agreement? It has been described as actually an investment agreement, not a trade agreement. If it were a free trade agreement, it would simply be one page long: Eliminate all barriers to trade and investment. But it is thousands of pages and contains volumes of tariff schedules. It is more complicated than that. It is an attempt to reduce the barriers to trade and investment among three countries of North America, gradually, openly, and hopefully, eliminate them. But, of course, as soon as you begin to think hard about non-tariff barriers, you begin to realize that eliminating them is a far more complicated act. Think of a non-tariff barrier as any government policy that assists one's exports or impedes one's imports, and you begin to realize that includes everything from health care to a sales tax on liquor in Minnesota to subsidies on wood products to agriculture price supports. It includes virtually all policies. Therefore, the question is not to eliminate all policies; some are very important and very useful, regulating safety and standards. One does not want to eliminate all standards; it would be better to harmonize policies so that one does not provide any particular advantage. Even then one runs into serious problems of taxation, which Canada may impose for one purpose, while some Americans feel that Canadians' health care is an unfair subsidy. So a North American Free Trade Agreement is more than a free trade agreement; it involves the *integration* of three very different countries in the fullest sense of that term.

Whose idea was NAFTA? The idea goes back to Simon Bolivar in the sense of his vision of hemisphere unity. A more specific source was James G. Blaine, Secretary of State in the 1880s in the United States, who called a conference in Washington for all of the foreign ministers of the Americas. One of the topics on the agenda was a customs union. He did not get very far, but sure enough, like all good ideas, one hundred years later, Carlos Salinas proposed a similar, more concrete idea. Salinas, who initially believed that free trade between the United States and Mexico was a terrible idea, changed his mind. I know because I had a long-running dialogue with Salinas. We went to graduate school together, and I knew what his views were because in the late 1970s when I was on the National Security Council, I broached some of these ideas with him, and he said, in typical Salinas fashion, "I had already thought about it and rejected it." But he changed his mind, and the question is why. I spoke with him at some length at that time, and I think the basic reason has to do with the debt crisis.

Again, if I can draw from Winston Churchill as my favorite quote-master, in 1945 after winning World War II, he lost the election. He went home, and his wife tried to console him: "Winnie, don't worry, losing the election was actually a blessing in disguise." To which he responded, "If it is a blessing, it is certainly well disguised." The debt crisis was a blessing in disguise. It was well disguised for the large majority of Latin Americans, who had to pay for the mishandling of their economies, but it was a blessing in the sense that it compelled a generation of new leaders to rethink their development strategy, to realize that the development strategy that they had pursued since the end of the war, the import-substitution-industrialization strategy was not working. They learned that a very different development strategy was working in Asia, based on exports, trade liberalization, a redefinition of the role of the state in the state's economy, and they adopted what became known as a "new consensus." That new consensus required first balancing the budget. In the case of Mexico, Salinas inherited a fiscal deficit of roughly 11.7 percent of GDP, which he halved in one year and by 1991 he was running a surplus, which he maintained. He reduced inflation from roughly 167 percent to single digits in his last year in office. He renegotiated the debt and managed it so well that he reduced it as a percentage of the GDP by nearly half, a task the United States has not even walked up to. As a signal of the kind of political leadership that he offered, particularly during the first five years of his administration, the comparison with what we have been able to do in the United States is quite astonishing. He sold 1100 para-statal corporations. He restored growth and, of course, re-attracted capital.

At the beginning of his administration, as all Mexicans have tended to do when faced with an economic problem or crisis, he looked away from the United States. He wanted to try to diversify relations. He went to Europe in 1989 and then to Japan to see whether they might be interested in opening their markets to Mexican goods and working out a freer trade system and invest in Mexico, but he found neither region interested. Europe at that time was self-preoccupied as it was after World War I and after World War II and is now after the Cold War. Europe was deepening and transforming its community into a European Union and in widening it to incorporate Eastern Europe. Japan was mostly focused on east Asia, and was sensitive to the U.S. concerns as it related to Mexico.

So Salinas did something genuinely revolutionary by Mexican standards: he proposed a free trade area with the United States. "Revolutionary" because it reversed 150 years of Mexican history. To maintain their culture and their autonomy, Mexicans had kept the United States at a distance, at arm's length, sometimes frustrating, sometimes infuriating the United States, but Mexicans were in control in defining the "limits to friendship," the limits to integration. They built walls that not only protected their industries, but protected an oppressive political system, and kept the United States outside.

Salinas took the genuinely revolutionary act of deciding to dismantle those walls and extend his hand to the United States in a new and close relationship. We should not underestimate how significant that step was. In my own judgment, I think it was bold, courageous, and the time had come. Public opinion polls suggest that Mexicans' views toward the United States had been undergoing some change. There is still tremendous ambivalence in Mexico, as Canadians will understand, in dealing with such a rich and powerful neighbor which is so insensitive and so unaware of their own concerns whereas every Mexican and every Canadian wakes up every day knowing that the elephant is next door and that some unintentional decision by some congressman in Iowa can have a profound impact on their lives in a way that no Mexican can have on an American. Those are all good reasons historically to build barriers, but Salinas was wise enough to understand that was not working anymore and that a different relationship was needed.

In the history of U.S.-Mexican relations, it is fascinating that whenever one side tries something bold and new, the other side reverses roles. And that is to a great extent what has happened in the last couple of years. George Bush's initial response to NAFTA was caution. Only when some Texas businessmen approached him and helped him to understand why it was such a great idea did he go ahead with it. But in a certain sense, he was also reflecting the ambivalence of America, which we saw so vividly during the NAFTA debate. As talks between the United States and Mexico began, Canada interrupted, saying, in effect: "Wait a second; we'd like to be at the table as well. Moreover, instead of two bilateral agreements -- United States-Canada and United States-Mexico -- let's have one North American agreement." Both Bush and Salinas were wise enough to understand the logic and sensitivity at work and so they all sat down at the table in 1991 and began negotiations, a negotiation that seemed simple at first but proved very complicated. It dragged on until the week before the Republican convention when President Bush announced that an agreement was reached in principle. Now why that particular moment? Obviously he already had a stake politically in NAFTA; he couldn't retreat from it, but the Democrats had a problem with NAFTA because the nature of the Democratic constituency places greater emphasis on two concerns that are largely outside the Republican political constellation: labor and the working man and the environment. Both groups had reservations about a North American trade agreement. By pushing this during the election, Bush was putting Clinton in an awkward position. Clinton tried to avoid the issue, particularly because there still was not a signed agreement, but finally on 8 October 1992, he gave a speech in which he came out in favor of NAFTA. But Clinton said that for such an agreement to be sustainable, it needs to incorporate the concerns of labor and the environment, perhaps in side agreements. More importantly, it needs to be part of the national economic strategy. Free trade benefits our whole country, but that does not mean it benefits everybody in the country and those who benefit need to figure out how to share those benefits with those who have to pay the price of increased competition. That was the idea. In December 1992 the agreement was finally ready for signature, and President Bush signed it. When President Clinton came into office he negotiated the two side agreements. They were signed in September 1993, and the agreement was approved by Congress in November 1993.

NAFTA already had a profound effect on regional integration by stimulating it and by serving as sort of a magnet for Latin American countries to begin to consider reducing their own barriers. One sees this most profoundly in the case of Mercosur -- Brazil, Argentina, Uruguay and Paraguay -- but also even the Andean Pact and the Central American Common Market. The culmination in many ways of NAFTA could be seen in the summit. What was so significant about the summit was not just the declared goal creating a free trade agreement in the whole of the Americas by 2005; it reflected a convergence of values in the hemisphere with regard to both political and economic regimes; a political regime around democratization, and accountability as something in which each country's leaders have to be elected by its people -- an old idea but not one with a long history in the rest of the Americas, and an economic regime around a market economy.

Former baseball manager Casey Stengel once said, "I never like to make predictions, especially about the future." I followed the debate on NAFTA in Congress very closely and heard many predictions but dare say that I do not recall anybody predicting that the day on which NAFTA came into force would be the day in which revolution would erupt in Chiapas. But, of course, that was the first supposed effect of NAFTA. Of course, these two events were not as closely linked as they seemed to be in the mind of Subcommandante Marcos, the Zapatista leader in Chiapas. The more profound impact of NAFTA followed the predictions of NAFTA's advocates. It accelerated trade. In just the first ten months of 1994, trade increased roughly in North America by 22 percent, quite a dramatic change. The impact on investment, both in anticipation of NAFTA and subsequently, was very great. Obviously there were other factors at work in 1994 in Mexico which led to the tremendous devaluation that occurred.

What was the impact on jobs? Those who argued that NAFTA would create jobs while NAFTA was considered by Congress felt confirmed in their analysis by the dramatic increase in exports by the United States since NAFTA came into effect. Those who were opposed to NAFTA because of the fear of loss of jobs calculate the numbers differently. My own personal view is that debate misses the point. It is not that NAFTA's effect on jobs is unimportant; it is terribly important. Rather, it is that NAFTA is about increasing competition, and in circumstances of increased competition, there are firms that win and jobs are created, and there are firms that lose in which jobs are lost. The real questions for the overall economy is, "Is competition beneficial or not?" In my judgment, it is beneficial even though it has costs, but it requires a recognition on the part of the state that those who lose need some safety net. Jobs are being created that pay a little bit more, that require more skills, more information, more technology, and unskilled jobs may be lost. The overall trajectory of the economy is moving in the right direction.

Psychologically, NAFTA's effect was quite real right up until 20 December 1994. Latin America had gotten a boost, a feeling that the region was climbing into the first world. I had just returned from a trip to Mexico. It was my first trip in more than a year; I was quite struck by how Mexico had changed. I have been visiting Mexico for 20 years, and others may not see it when they are there every day. I could see a major change. I could see it in the buildings that had been constructed, and in the streets. That was evident in the Summit of the Americas in December.

The effect on politics and democratization in Mexico was more subtle. The electoral process of 1994 in Mexico was not a totally clean, fair, and equitable process as has occurred in every other country in the hemisphere with the exception of Cuba and the Dominican Republic. Those are the only three countries in the hemisphere that have had flawed elections in the last few years, but nonetheless Mexico made progress during this last year in the electoral process -- in the registration, in creating greater independence for the elections commission, in assuring more verification of the registration list, and in the vote and count. There were quick counts to determine that. There were a lot of indicators that the electoral process took an important step forward in Mexico in the last year, a very important leap forward, but it had not yet reached the nirvana of an unflawed electoral process. There is still a credibility gap that needs to be closed. I think part of the reason they took that step forward, however, was because of the openness of the North American relationship. The fact is that U.S. citizens, Canadians, and the world were watching that election more closely than ever before. They were not willing to tolerate and accept the kind of manipulation that had occurred in the past. And Mexicans themselves were unwilling to tolerate it. They got out and they organized independent monitoring mechanisms. As many as 88,000 Mexicans went out to watch their own elections and to try to keep it honest in a way that would not have occurred before, and I think that is related to NAFTA in an indirect way. Knowing that the world was watching, Mexicans were going to take their own election more seriously. I always found it interesting in Mexico that so many of my Mexican friends would only take seriously an event that had occurred in Mexico when they read it in the New York Times, or when they watched it on CBS news. At that moment, local events affect them. The fact that NAFTA had passed, and the world was watching the election, began a process hopefully irreversible that will lead to the opening of what had been historically an extremely opaque political system.

NAFTA had an important, albeit indirect effect on the region's trade and markets. Trade within the Andean Pact tripled; within MERCOSUR, it doubled. Regional integration had a long-standing history but it had never really done anything. In the few years since NAFTA was first proposed, Latin America has moved forward quite dramatically, and trade has increased in an astonishing way in the Americas.

What has its effect been on world trade? There were some people who had argued that if we approve NAFTA, it would be a stumbling block to approving GATT; it would send a signal to the Japanese and the Europeans that we are going to build a fortress around the hemisphere. I did not believe that was to be the case; I actually believed the opposite would happen, and I am pleased that prediction succeeded. I had felt that first of all, the United States and the large trading countries in the world are simply too interdependent, we are too tied to the international economy to think that you can create regional trading blocs. There had been a GATT negotiation underway since 1986, but it had stagnated. The greatest market in the world remains the United States, and indeed it was the fear ultimately by Canada of being locked out of the U.S. market, then by Mexico of being locked out of the U.S. market, that compelled them to accelerate a process of trade liberalization and integration, and indeed, that is exactly what happened as a result of NAFTA. The Europeans and the Japanese who had been extremely complacent about their access to the U.S. market began to take more seriously the idea that the United States may have another option in North America. It is not at all a surprise to me, in fact, I predicted that if NAFTA were approved that within months, certainly within a year, the GATT would accelerate and be approved and that is, of course, what happened and now we have the GATT approved and the World Trade Organization taking shape.

What effect has NAFTA had on environment and labor? Well, the truth is that the side agreements have been very slow in taking shape and so it is simply too soon to assess whether it has had much of a positive effect on those areas. But I think we need to continue to look at that.

What effect has it had on the internal economies of the three nations? It has had a modest boost for Canada, trade has increased, employment has increased. It has had a modest effect on the United States, the most modest for obvious reasons, in that for the largest economy, trade is the least important as compared to our two neighbors but it has been a modest, positive effect. Its effect on Mexico is more serious and much more complicated. It has lifted the country as a whole, or at least it did so up until December 1994, and it will do so again. But it has perhaps exacerbated some inequalities. Trade may play that role in the absence of a government role to compensate for this increased competition. All three countries are facing widening income gaps. President Clinton has done some very important steps to addressing that, first through the income tax on the top 2 percent, secondly by the earned income tax credits for the lower 20 or 30 percent, thirdly, by education in investment and training. These things are helping, but the trends in technology and trade are actually working against us. They are widening this gap between income groups. Not enough is being done about it. Indeed, it seems to be even worse. Very little is even being spoken about that. But certainly in a place like Mexico where the number who are marginalized or impoverished vastly exceeds anything comparable in the United States or in Canada, widening income gaps are far more dangerous and much more serious.

Finally, what effect has NAFTA had on financing? That gets us to the peso crisis. There was a degree of financial integration which simply was ignored by NAFTA and as a result, the United States and Mexico are paying a price-- Mexico in particular, the United States just in excess dollars. When I was in Mexico a friend of mine who always comes up with a joke for every tragedy in Mexico asked me how much did I think the US$50 billion represented in old pesos, and I tried to calculate. He said, "Don't worry. The answer is very simple. All of them." This is a major crisis and the question we need to think about is does it represent a failure of NAFTA, a success of NAFTA, or that NAFTA was inadequate? We have heard the arguments of those who argue that it represents a failure of NAFTA. It's obvious. The magnitude of the collapse, the dependency of Mexico -- this was no panacea. It is hard to make that argument or at least to connect it to NAFTA. I think a more plausible argument is that it actually reflects more the success of NAFTA. What happened in Mexico was a consequence of very rapid, accelerated integration in trade between the two countries, and a current account deficit that simply got out of hand for a number of reasons, both political and economic. So in a certain sense, it is a product of the success of NAFTA. But it is also a sign of the inadequacy of NAFTA because NAFTA really was a product of dynamic integration. One manifestation of that is financial integration and yet no institution, no procedure, no consultative device was set up to cope with or to anticipate that form of integration. Everybody knew that the peso was overvalued. Yet did the U.S. Treasury or the Federal Reserve send somebody to meet with President Salinas or President-elect Zedillo and say, "You better act on this soon, because if you don't act on this soon, we are all going to have to pay a higher price?" The answer is no. Nobody did, and that should have been a part of NAFTA.

Let me provide some figures to give you some sense of the implications of what I think is happening in the hemisphere on trade. First, trade with Mexico has really expanded quite dramatically over time: U.S. exports from Mexico increased from US$5 billion in 1975 to over US$41 billion in 1993 and up to almost US$50 billion in 1994. For a very long time Americans have focused on Europe and more recently on Asia, but let me just give you some sense of their relative importance as opposed to all of North America. It is not significant. From 1955 U.S. exports, to our two neighbors, Canada and Mexico, already exceeded exports to the European Community and to Japan and East Asia. Now take a look at 1994. U.S. exports to Mexico and Canada are 60 percent higher than those to the European Union and still significantly more than to Japan and Southeast Asia. Everybody knows that Canada is our largest and most important trading partner, but in 1994 Mexico came very close to Japan as being as important a market for U.S. goods. There is discussion about who can purchase US$50 billion worth of American exports, whether it just goes to the top 2 percent. If you think of it in per capita terms, per capita imports from the United States by Mexico exceed by more than a factor of 10 per capita imports from Japan, and exceed per capita imports from Germany, and even from the U.K. Indeed in terms of per capita basis of imports, Mexicans purchase more (despite their poverty) from the United States on a one-on-one basis than any other country in the world with the exception of Canada. Now, of course, this does not necessarily mean consumer products. We are talking about aggregate figures. But even if you look at consumer products, the results are quite startling. There is a large poorer population in Mexico, but there are also a lot of television sets and there is a lot of consumer goods, and a growing middle class.

The next point I want to make is with regard to regional trade. While global trade is increasing in the world, trade within regions is increasing at a far more rapid rate, and that is not just the case of the European Union, as you would expect. Nearly 56 percent of all of the trade of the countries of the European Union is with each other. But startling, however, is that in 1994, within the three countries of North America, 47.4 percent -- nearly half -- of all of the trade that the three countries of North America do in the world is with each other. So you are not talking about a trading bloc but you are talking about regions, regions that are developing, and North America is as significant a region as that of the European Union and far more so than we are seeing in Asia. Integration, in short, is increasing at a very rapid rate.

Now, of course, that integration is not symmetrical. Mexico and Canada are obviously far more dependent on the United States than the United States is on them. In 1993 only 30.5 percent of U.S. trade is with North America as opposed to 84 percent of Mexico's trade being with North America, and nearly 80 percent of Canada. But still for an economy the size of the United States, nearly one-third of its trade is with its two neighbors, and 47 percent for all of North America does signify a very integrated region. And indeed, if you broke that down by subregions in the United States -- if you looked at the southwest and its integration with Mexico or you looked at the midwest and its integration with Canada -- you would see it more profoundly.

Finally, what happens if you expand NAFTA to all of the hemisphere? What does that mean? Even with just the very fewest steps to liberalize trade, U.S. exports to North and South America in 1994 were nearly US$200 billion. That's almost twice U.S. exports to the European Union, and that is even before South America really begins to liberalize its trade because the first steps that it has taken are still quite modest. We are still at a very early stage with regard to trying to press NAFTA into a hemispheric union.

What conclusions can we draw from that? I think North America is already a formidable region, a highly integrated region in which trade is increasingly important to the three countries and that trade is not just products. It is services, it is ideas, it is education, it is culture, it is finance, it is our societies as a whole.

Second, NAFTA is inadequate to deal with an integration process as dynamic as is occurring right now. And the consequence of that inadequacy should be seen in the lesson of the peso collapse. We will see repeated problems and failures, whether it is called Proposition 187 or the collapse of the peso or a drug trafficking problem on the border. These events will seem quite dissimilar, quite distinct, but they all are related to an integration process for which we just have not yet begun to change our minds to understand how they are in fact connected in a way that will permit us to resolve them without each one becoming a crisis.

Finally, I think the time has come not to put up barriers. It may be a time for reflection, a time for correction but not to put up barriers. The time has come to try to accelerate the movement toward freer trade, widen it and also consider ways to deepen it in order to mitigate some of the adverse consequences that I mentioned. Lily Tomlin once said, "Together, we are in this alone." That really is a good way to summarize this book, of standing apart but recognizing that we are a part of a larger unit. Each of the three countries will try to maintain its sense of autonomy and identity while at the same time dismantling barriers. President Salinas, while he is being vilified in Mexico right now, still was very much a revolutionary precisely because he understood that sovereignty is not some firm, irreversible, immutable concept. It is an idea that evolves, that matures, that is transformed, that can be stretched and extended. To maintain one's sense of identity, sometimes you erect a wall, but if you want to enhance your sense of nationhood, you need to compete, you need to be a part of the world, you need to bring the barriers down. You need to reach across to your neighbors and if you do so, you can grow a great deal more. It is easy to stay behind fences, but growth is not really possible behind fences. One needs to reach across.

I started with Churchill, and let me end with Churchill. The question is whether we will go forward, and I think that is a good question. There is fatigue in the United States, there is demoralization in Mexico, there is continued ambivalence and division within Canada. The rest of the hemisphere is frightened by the potential, ripple effect of the peso. In Argentina and elsewhere, investors are like lemmings, they moved in as a wave without thinking, and they are moving out without thinking. There is a good reason to feel a pall of pessimism, but I do not want to end on a pessimistic note. Winston Churchill had it right when he said of Americans, "I have faith in Americans" he said, "Americans ..." (and here I want to broaden it to reflect the three nations) "North Americans ..." (and Mexicans are going to have to rethink their word Norte Americano because they are now North Americans as well) "North Americans," Churchill said, "always choose the right decision. Unfortunately, it is only after they have exhausted all the other possibilities."

Robert A. Pastor

PREFACE

The Dean Rusk Center for International and Comparative Law and the Department of Political Science at the University of Georgia cosponsored a two-day conference "Joining Together, Standing Apart: National Identities After NAFTA" at the University of Georgia. This conference brought together an interdisciplinary group of scholars from the fields of international law, political science, sociology, and economics to discuss the ramifications of the North American Free Trade Agreement (NAFTA) for greater integration of the national identities of Canada, the United States, and Mexico. It is the contributed papers from this conference which comprise the chapters of this book.

The conference focused on three areas affected by the move toward integration which NAFTA represents: economic integration, cultural sovereignty, and environmental sustainability. The contributing authors provide a comparative analysis of the differing impacts that trade has on Canada, the United States, and Mexico.

The book examines the initial stages of the NAFTA experience and evaluates the long-term implications of this agreement beyond those of ending trade and tariff barriers among the three signatories. NAFTA initiated a procedure for addressing transborder economic problems more adequately and in a more predictable fashion. It does not come close to the wide-ranging integration proposed under the single European Act. Yet NAFTA does hold the promise for encouraging policy convergence between three disparate political cultures.

If the globalization of the world economy produces integrative forces, one would expect parochial domestic issues to fade as this integration proceeds. Yet there are asymmetries which contradict this expectation. The liberalization of Mexican investment policy means greater opportunity for foreign (particularly U.S.) economic expansion into that nation. To the north, Quebec nationalists view NAFTA as providing an opportunity for the province to achieve recognition of its identity, thereby reinforcing this regional identity internationally. On the other hand, the large percentage of industry controlled by Americans renders Canadian economic policy highly sensitive to U.S. developments.

Typically, free trade agreements like NAFTA touch upon many domestic policy issues which affect economic activity. The internationalization of production requires convergence of domestic policies out of considerations of practicality, economic efficiency, and competitive fairness. While practicality and economic efficiency are fairly straightforward concepts, competitive fairness is more complex than it may appear at first glance. Competitive fairness, or the "level playing field" concept, requires all players in the competition to accept market outcomes. Yet the acceptance of such outcomes has been developed traditionally in a national context, based on a national set of regulations covering economic, social, and environmental regulations.

Cross-border integration enmeshes these national economies more deeply, and is accompanied by a greater need for coordination of microeconomic policies. Rather than address the economic, social, and environmental policy issues separately, trade policy now serves as the vehicle for negotiating this policy convergence. As a consequence, trade officials are being forced to address an expanded array of domestic policy issues.

Beyond the economic aspects of NAFTA, the book addresses the less studied cultural implications of this new international arrangement. How has NAFTA affected key regional, ethnic, and political groupings within Canada, Mexico, and the United States? Contributors to this portion of the book probe advantages and disadvantages posed by NAFTA with respect to the healing of cultural breaches within the boundaries of signatory nations. NAFTA's meaning for the Quebec separatist movement is one focus. Another is the Mexican dilemma of uneven regional development and the accompanying tensions between Mexico City and the hinterland, especially the Indian population in Chiapas and other poverty-stricken areas. The U.S. problems of immigration burdens on border states to the south and Native American disaffections in border states to the north provide additional topics that warrant examination. Have attempts at economic integration spurred steps toward cultural integration as well, or simply exacerbated old conflicts?

Environmental protection and conservation issues have come to the forefront of the international political agenda. Although nations generally recognize the problems and agree on the ultimate goal of protecting the environment, countries remain divided on the issue of how to approach and remedy the problems. A major reason why nations have been unable to agree on a unified approach is the existence of sovereignty concerns that are unique to the environmental area. In the environment context, sovereignty has come to symbolize the ability to control territory and the natural resources located within the territory; the right to choose the manner in which natural resources are exploited; and the state's authority to create its own policy to regulate the environment.

There are a number of prominent historical examples of these conflicts in the North American context, particularly in the area of fisheries. Mexico and the United States have clashed over the inadvertent killing of dolphins caught in tuna-fishing operations in the eastern Pacific and Canada and the United States have disagreed over lobster and salmon fisheries. However, cooperation and collaboration, especially in the U.S.-Canada context, have outweighed collisions between sovereigns. On the other hand, it was the perception that Mexico might gain a competitive advantage by providing a "pollution haven" of low environmental standards more attractive to industries than the United States or Canada that propelled the NAFTA signatories toward a degree of harmonization in environmental regulations.

By setting up a trilateral panel to evaluate environmental standards on competitiveness grounds, NAFTA's environmental side agreement created a new way to address environmental concerns while protecting local standards, once again illustrating the attempt to achieve policy convergence by means of a trade apparatus. As in other areas covered in the book, NAFTA represents the continuing tension between integration and the maintenance of national autonomy.

Dorinda G. Dallmeyer
University of Georgia
Athens, Georgia

ACKNOWLEDGEMENTS

I wish to express my appreciation to Loch K. Johnson, Regents Professor of Political Science at the University of Georgia, for his collaboration on the conference which resulted in this volume. He was instrumental in crafting grant proposals as well as deftly administering conference logistics.

I gratefully acknowledge financial support by the Canadian Studies Grant Program, Canadian Embassy, Washington, D.C. and other assistance provided by the Canadian Consulate General in Atlanta, Georgia. Consul General Allan Stewart and Ms. Judith Costello have provided a great deal of encouragement for the endeavors of the Rusk Center with regard to Canada; I look forward to continuing this collaboration in the future.

Additional funding to support the conference was provided by the State-of-the-Art Conference Grant Program, Office of the Vice President for Academic Affairs, University of Georgia. I wish to acknowledge Dean Edward D. Spurgeon of the University of Georgia School of Law for underwriting this conference as well as the support of Professor Thomas J. Schoenbaum, Executive Director of the Dean Rusk Center for International and Comparative Law. Dr. Thomas Lauth, head of the Department of Political Science, also assisted with funding for the conference. The International Trade and Environment Project of the Georgia Consortium on Negotiation and Conflict Resolution supported research related to this book. The cooperation of the American Society of International Law in designating the conference a regional meeting of the Society is gratefully acknowledged.

The production of a manuscript is a demanding task. Ms. Deval R. Karina Zaveri, J.D. University of Georgia 1997, assisted with last-minute research needs. Special thanks go to Ms. Nelda Parker of the Dean Rusk Center who remains incomparable not only for her skill, attention to detail, and efficiency, but also for her unfailing good humor.

Finally, thanks go to R. David Dallmeyer for his patience, understanding, and encouragement.

Chapter One

NAFTA AND ECONOMIC INTEGRATION:
THREE PERSPECTIVES

by Louis L. Ortmayer

The debate over the...North American Free Trade Agreement has taken on an astonishing salience in American politics. Not since the Smoot-Hawley tariff has trade legislation produced such a bitter polarization of opinion.

--Paul Krugman[1]

1. INTRODUCTION

It is not surprising that NAFTA has occasioned wide debate and strong passions in the United States given the significance of Mexico in this country's foreign and international economic policies. Mexico is the third most important trading partner for the United States, after Canada and Japan. It is the United States' most important foreign source of petroleum and the third best market for U.S. agricultural products. Mexico is also one of the leading countries in Latin America in terms of U.S. foreign investment. Moreover, cooperation with Mexico is vital in dealing with a whole range of collateral issues of high priority for United States foreign policy, including coping with illegal immigration, stemming the flow of illicit drugs to the United States, environmental pollution, and a host of border problems.

---

[1] Krugman, "The Uncomfortable Truth about NAFTA: It's Foreign Policy, Stupid," 72 *Foreign Aff.* 13 (Nov./Dec. 1993).

1

D. G. Dallmeyer (ed.), Joining Together, Standing Apart: National Identities after NAFTA, 1–34.
© 1997 *Kluwer Law International. Printed in the Netherlands.*

With these vital interests in mind, it is possible to downplay the economic significance of NAFTA to focus primarily on its implications for foreign relations. Indeed, one leading economist has stated that NAFTA's economic benefits will be real, but small, and its labor and environmental costs, those issues that so inflamed the public discourse through public figures like Ross Perot, will be minimal.

One might then ask: Why should the Clinton Administration expend a great deal of its depleted political capital in pursuit of an unpopular and economically trivial agreement? The answer is that Mexico's government needs NAFTA, and the United States has a strong interest in helping their government.[2]

While Krugman's contentions may be true, this chapter asserts that NAFTA is more than just foreign policy, or the calculated pursuit of the national interest. NAFTA, viewed from the United States, is the complex process by which contending forces of economic liberalization and protectionism have struck a temporary compromise. In addition, it is the complicated product of an evolutionary postwar U.S. trade policy that is still changing from a long-term basis in multilateral economic liberalism to an amalgam of multilateral, regional, bilateral, and protectionist elements.

This study will briefly highlight the contributions of three analytical perspectives which individually and in concert illuminate the complex underpinnings of NAFTA. NAFTA can be seen as a form of the dialectic acting on U.S. international economic and trade policy. NAFTA also fits comfortably into the analytical framework of "two-level games," the result of a complex diplomatic and political bargaining process conducted simultaneously at the international and domestic levels. Thirdly, the subnational actors perspective, filtered through the viewpoint of multinational corporate strategy, pinpoints the widely divergent impact of NAFTA on key industries and economic sectors in North America. These perspectives together assert that NAFTA is both politics and economics, and that the political economy of NAFTA should be viewed as both process and policy, each of which is dynamic and continuously evolving.

---

[2]   *Id.* at 18. In the context of trade policy, the use of the term Hegelian dialectic signifies the process by which innovations in trade liberalization are countered by innovations in protectionism and are succeeded by some synthesis that is temporarily acceptable to each of the competing sides, followed by yet another innovation in liberalization, countered by yet another innovation in protectionism, followed by yet another synthesis, and so on.

2. NAFTA: ECONOMIC INTEGRATION OR POLICY DIALECTIC?

The first perspective on NAFTA takes an approach which focuses on the interaction of trade policy and negotiation processes as a variation of a dialectic. Some analysts have considered the NAFTA agreements part of a larger economic integration process that goes beyond narrowly defined trade policy.[3] Because of the initiatives of the United States, issues with only tenuous direct connections to trade have come under negotiation in NAFTA. In this view, a harmonization of national policies that appears tantamount to a broad movement toward integration seems under way. But is such a movement verifiable? NAFTA clearly makes trade freer on a broad front among the three signatories, and it will probably bring about the efficiency enhancements typical of trade liberalization. On closer look, however, one can argue that in many respects what may at first look like integration appears on further scrutiny more as a form of (Hegelian) dialectic over trade policy.[4]

In order to argue that a dialectical progression appropriately characterizes what has taken place in the NAFTA negotiations, and the accompanying parallel agreements, and why economic integration seems not a fully appropriate characterization, some background perspective is necessary. This section first considers the antecedents of the NAFTA negotiations, with events that precipitated NAFTA beginning in the 1970s at the very latest.

2.1   EVOLUTION OF U.S. TRADE POLICY: CONFLICT AND INNOVATION

U.S. trade policy, from the Bretton Woods treaties until the late 1970s, was grounded on an unconditional interpretation of the most favored nation (MFN) provision of the General Agreement on Tariffs and Trade (GATT).[5] The United

---

[3]   For example, see Pastor, "NAFTA as the Center of an Integration Process: The Non-trade Issues," in N. Lustig, B.P. Bosworth, & R.Z. Lawrence (eds.), *North American Free Trade: Assessing the Impact* 176-198 (1992); Weintraub, "The North American Free Trade Agreement as Negotiated: A U.S. Perspective," in S. Globerman & M. Walker (eds.), *Assessing NAFTA: A Trinational Analysis* (1993).

[4]   For an analysis that describes NAFTA as a game that leads to a dialectical progression, see Gruben, "North American Free Trade: Opportunities and Pitfalls," 10 *Contemp. Issues* 1-10 (Oct. 1992). For an approach that poses the evolution of financial regulation in the same way, see Kane, "Interaction of Financial and Regulatory Innovation," 78 *Am. Econ. Rev.* 328-334 (May 1988).

[5]   The MFN clause requires a member country that lowers tariffs on specific products from a specific country to then lower them to all member nations of GATT. Throughout this era the U.S. consistently argued against the preferential status ("special and differential

States was the principal proponent of such a multilateral approach to international trade liberalization. But by the late 1970s, the United States had become frustrated with GATT. The sources of frustration for the United States were the following: the caravan effect (GATT negotiations emulate a caravan that moves only as fast as its slowest camel), the free rider problem (some countries, chiefly the developing states, have benefited from the multilateral system, without reciprocating by lowering substantially their own barriers), and the rise of trade-related issues not covered by GATT, such as direct foreign investment, trade in services, agriculture, and intellectual property rights.[6] The confluence of these strands of irritation over time had an impact on trade policy makers and resulting trade policy.

While the caravan effect is fairly obvious, the free rider and trade-related issues problems deserve further amplification. Although many countries had joined GATT seeking to open foreign markets, they were often less willing to open their own. For the developing countries (LDCs), whose competitive positions in many industries were unfavorable *vis-à-vis* the industrialized world, this protectionist predisposition was considered understandable. GATT provided special reservations for the LDCs and offered them special openings to the developed states under the generalized system of preferences (GSP). But for some countries, these special provisions were not enough, as they utilized the particular nature of GATT to their own protectionist advantage.

GATT had been designed to lower tariffs, as tariffs had been the protectionist instrument of choice before World War II. Over time, many GATT members simply replaced their tariffs barriers with other, GATT-legal forms of protection. Quantitative restrictions (quotas and permits) became commonplace, as did regulations and standards restrictions, such as "product quality" provisions. Export subsidies proliferated, while detailed regulations against direct foreign investment appeared. Intellectual piracy mounted, as some countries became safe havens through weak patent and copyright protections, seeking to become centers of unlicensed production.[7]

These innovations in protectionism multiplied during the 1980s, especially in the developing countries, in response to the decline in primary commodity prices, to terms-of-trade shocks, and to the subsequent foreign debt problems of many of the LDCs. Throughout the 1980s, the prices of the LDCs' traditional

treatment") accorded developing countries in the interests of economic development.
[6]   *Cf.* J.J. Schott, *The Global Trade Negotiations: What Can Be Achieved?* (1990); I.M. Destler, *American Trade Politics* (3d ed., 1995); D. Tussie & D. Glover (eds.), *The Developing Countries in World Trade: Policies and Bargaining Strategies* (1993).
[7]   *See* J.J. Schott, *The Uruguay Round: An Assessment* 77-99 (1994).

raw materials exports experienced a prolonged slump, bringing on huge balance of payments deficits, which the developing states in turn sought to finance by means of international borrowing. To respond to these pressures, LDCs adopted philosophies and trade policies more akin to economic nationalism or neo-mercantilism than to GATT, using GATT-legal nontariff innovations at their core.

In the meantime, certain technological developments caused the United States to come to regard these rising new barriers as particularly odious. Revolutions in communications and transportation encouraged production-sharing arrangements and the globalization of production, while also promoting opportunities for U.S. trade in services abroad. These developments prompted the United States to pressure its trading partners to open their markets and allow the expansion of such trade.

This conjunction of opposing forces, factors making trade openings more attractive to the United States at the same time the LDCs and other countries' innovations in protectionism were raising trade barriers, led the United States to launch a program of what came to be called "aggressive reciprocity."[8] The United States responded with trade policy adaptations of its own. Section 301 of the 1974 Trade Act and its subsequent revision, "Super 301," of the Omnibus Trade and Competitiveness Act of 1988, allowed the United States new maneuverability in threatening trade retaliations. The United States used these threat instruments to extract trade openings from other countries, as well as to induce trade partners to modify their policies such as tightening intellectual property protection. A case in point is the dispute between the United States and Brazil over informatics or computer software.

But protectionists also quickly contrived to use these same U.S. trade innovations for quite different purposes than opening foreign markets. For instance, the United States utilized Section 301 and Super 301 to negotiate "voluntary" export restraints (VERs), another U.S. innovation in protectionism in which exporting countries "volunteer" to restrict their exports to the United States. Foreign trade partners slow in volunteering soon faced the threat of 301-based trade sanctions. The United States also dramatically increased its countervailing actions, such as raising duties against countries it charged with dumping or other "unfair" trade practices. Studies have demonstrated the merits of many of these charges to have been questionable at best.[9]

---

[8] *Cf.* T.O. Bayard & K.A. Elliott, *Reciprocity and Retaliation in U.S. Trade Policy* (1994).

[9] *Cf.* G.C. Hufbauer, D.E. Berliner, & K.A. Elliott, *Trade Protection in the United*

To summarize, in the context of U.S. trade policy, the 1970s and 1980s saw two types of dialectics at work. The first involved a dialectic between those groups in the United States who wanted free trade abroad (open markets) but not so much at home, and foreign countries who also wanted free trade for others but not so much for their home markets. That is, as one side developed trade policy innovations in forms of both liberalization and protectionism, they were countered and complemented by the innovations of the other side.

Secondly, the realignments in international trade patterns that inspired the U.S. initiatives through the GATT in the Uruguay Round also altered who wanted protectionism and who did not. Some U.S. industries which had favored protectionism in the past discovered that changes in production technologies, communications, and in markets had made free trade more beneficial and therefore more agreeable. Other traditional protectionists found that these very changes favored increased protectionist efforts as well. Those firms involved in international production-sharing, exporting partially manufactured productions abroad for further processing and then importing the results for final processing at home, favored increased liberalization. On the other side of the dialectical process, U.S. labor unions viewed such sharing of production as signifying fewer union jobs in the United States, and they consequently stepped up both direct and indirect pressures toward restricting trade.

2.2   NAFTA AS THE NEXT STAGE

These shifting alliances and the redistribution of pressures for and against trade liberalization developed further in the establishment of the negotiating frameworks which would lead to NAFTA. The opportunities for a free trade agreement in North America had advanced with the internationalization of production and the waning of protectionist sentiment on the part of U.S. manufacturers. On the other hand, U.S. labor unions demanded the negotiation of parallel agreements--especially on the workplace, labor adjustment, and the environment--to avoid what they argued would become destructive competition.

The progress of the parallel negotiations and the intensity of the lobbying efforts involved with them strongly suggest that the protectionist camp saw them as a mechanism to sink the NAFTA itself. Protectionists ratcheted their demands upward, as agreements were reached, since they deemed none of the agreements adequate. Disparities occurring between U.S. and Mexican labor and environ-

States: 31 Case Studies (1986); Bayard & Elliott, *supra* note 8.

mental laws--or their enforcement--attracted charges of "social dumping."[10]

One major sticking point in the parallel negotiations suggests a great deal about whether the U.S. agenda involved economic integration or whether it reflected the protectionist side of a dialectical process. Although the United States, Mexico, and Canada all concurred that violation of the parallel agreements ought to incur penalties, the United States was alone in arguing that the penalties should include selected revivals of protectionism. Canadian and Mexican negotiators, perceiving a contradiction in the use of protectionism to achieve free trade, favored fines. In addition, some of NAFTA's provisions toward what some regard as integration can also be interpreted as attempts by U.S. protectionists to broaden their efforts against freer trade by pressing issues that the other two parties might have perceived as infringing on their national sovereignty.

The bottom line is that, from one perspective, the efforts of both pro- and anti-protectionist forces have jointly determined NAFTA, and they will assuredly determine together how the agreement will evolve over time. One more example may suffice to make the case here. In an attempt to secure the votes sufficient to ratify NAFTA, the Clinton administration entered into NAFTA-related agreements that were not a part of NAFTA, as in the case of the orange juice trade, in order to reerect barriers that NAFTA would have lowered.[11] A selective discussion of the NAFTA accords, its expected effects, and the political alignments that will influence its implementation may further highlight these competing forces.

2.3   NAFTA NEGOTIATIONS: LIBERALIZATION

While the parallel agreements certainly reflect both protectionist and liberalizing pressures, the NAFTA itself mirrors the same interplay of opposing ideas and political forces.

NAFTA does not free trade, but it obviously liberalizes it. Over a 15-year period, NAFTA progressively reduces and then eliminates all tariffs and most nontariff barriers between Canada, Mexico, and the United States. Moreover, NAFTA is a GATT-forward agreement; no signatories can increase their tariffs

---

[10]   AFL-CIO, *Policy Recommendations for 1992* (1992).
[11]   Cloud, "As NAFTA countdown begins, wheeling, dealing intensifies," *Cong. Q. Weekly Rep.* 3104-3107 (Nov. 13, 1993); Stokes, "A Hard Sell," *National Journal* 2472-2476 (Oct. 16, 1993); "NAFTA Crucible: Undecided members weigh voter fears as trade pact showdown approaches," *Cong. Q. Weekly Rep.* 3011-3022 (Nov. 6, 1993).

on imports from countries within or outside the free trade area. Although many goods entered the United States and Mexico duty-free prior to NAFTA, the accords eliminated many tariffs as soon as the agreements went into effect. (See Table I.) Further, NAFTA addresses much more than merchandise trade. The United States in particular secured its long-standing goals of liberalizing trade in services and foreign investment rules abroad, at least in this trinational context, and it tightened the protection of intellectual property rights. It is significant, moreover, that NAFTA represents an achievement the United States has had more difficulty realizing in a broader multilateral context.

Table 1 - NAFTA: Schedule on Tariff Elimination

Category Date	U.S. Imports from Mexico (Percent of total)	Mexican Imports from the U.S. (Percent of total)
Duty-free before agreement	13.9	17.9
Additional opening effective on NAFTA start data: Jan. 1, 1994.	53.8	31.0
Additional opening five years after	8.5	17.4
Additional opening ten years after	23.1	31.8
Additional opening fifteen years after	.7	1.4
Total Value	$28.9 billion	$14.2 billion

SOURCE: United States International Trade Commission, *Potential Impact on the U.S. Economy and Selected Industries of the North American Free-Trade Agreement* (Washington; USITC, January 1993), pp. 1-3.

Although NAFTA opens the markets of Canada and the United States, it has the greatest impact on the liberalization in Mexico. NAFTA especially broadens Canadian and American companies' ability to establish or purchase a business in Mexico, and it facilitates their selling of their assets should they decide to leave. NAFTA further relaxes previous restrictions on expanding business operations in Mexico, while removing restrictions on profit remittance to foreign countries. NAFTA eliminates local content requirements, although NAFTA-wide content rules will exist. Finally, NAFTA loosens restrictions on work permits and removes licensing and performance criteria.

2.4   ...AND PROTECTIONISM

Despite such substantial liberalization, however, NAFTA initially retains protectionist elements, some of which persist indefinitely. NAFTA protects sensitive sectors -- such as agriculture, minerals, banking, textiles, and apparel -- by stretching out the phase-in time. This protection is temporary.

But (dialectically) as the synthesis of liberal and protectionist pressures,

NAFTA contains other types of protection that are not only permanent but also raise trade barriers above pre-NAFTA levels.[12] In a number of key sectors -- notably automobiles, textiles, and apparel -- NAFTA imposes North American content rules, some of which will serve to increase protection. Under the 1989 U.S.-Canada Free Trade Agreement, for instance, one could import autos duty-free if they contained at least 50 percent Canadian-U.S. inputs. In order to receive NAFTA benefits, autos require 62.5 percent. For textiles and apparel to qualify for "free" trade under NAFTA, all components -- starting with the yarn or fiber -- must be made in North America. For the latter sector, the NAFTA covenant extends and strengthens the protectionism inherent in the broader, multinational Multifibre Agreement (MFA).

Thus, NAFTA unequivocally liberalizes trade in North America, but not across the board. The careful elaboration of domestic content requirements signals that protectionism has also found a place in NAFTA.

2.5   SECTORAL EFFECTS

The question arises, that if most studies of the potential impact of NAFTA suggest overall economic expansion for the United States,[13] why then did protectionists turn so much of their energy, and anger, against the U.S. government and threaten the ratification process? In a broad sense, the answer is that the opening up of trade shifts resources and production from less competitive to more competitive sectors, inspiring renewed and fierce political efforts from the less competitive.

Most studies indicate that the U.S. sectors which stand to lose include sugar refining, fruits and vegetables, apparel, and household appliances. Sectors that will gain include chemicals, instruments, machinery and equipment, motor vehicles, and rubber and plastics. Despite candidate Ross Perot's graphic warnings, neither the output or employment gains of the winners, nor the losses of the losers, appears likely to be large, according to the studies and a number of modeling efforts, but the probable losers find small comfort in such palliatives.

---

[12]   *See* Morici, "NAFTA Rules of Origin and Automotive Content Requirements;" Johnson, "NAFTA and the Trade in Automotive Goods;" and Barry & Sawicki, "NAFTA: The Textile and Apparel Sector," all in S. Globerman & M. Walker (eds.), *Assessing NAFTA: A Trinational Analysis* (1993); U.S. Int'l Trade Comm., Potential Impact on the U.S. Economy and Selected Industries of the North American Free Trade Agreement (1993).
[13]   *Cf.* J.J. Schott, "NAFTA: An American Perspective," 8 *Int'l Trade J.* 3-8 (Spring 1994); Conference Board of Canada, *North American Outlook: 1995-1996, A Research Report* (1995).

Finally, an obvious but important reason that reactive anti-liberalization lobbying has been strong -- regardless of the nature and benefits of the particular trade initiative (in this case NAFTA) -- is that it is easier for those who are likely to lose their jobs to know that this is probable, than for those who may gain jobs to know that they will be the ones to gain them. After all, even if the process of carving out a free trade area creates new jobs, someone else might get them. And NAFTA's intertwining of the trade agenda with environmental, labor, and human rights concerns reflects the product of a political convergence in the United States -- "a marriage of convenience between nongovernmental organizations that have learned to leverage the U.S. Congress and traditionally protectionist forces in the labor and business communities...The economic, political, and conceptual ramifications of conditioning trade to a complex social and political agenda are sufficiently thorny to provide grist for conflict, creativity, or stalemate."[14]

2.6   NAFTA AND BEYOND

Many of the traits of the NAFTA accords and the parallel negotiations are consistent with moves toward greater economic integration, leaving many analysts to conclude just that. But in the context of U.S. trade policy and trade history, they may also be viewed as part of a dialectical process in which shifting protectionist and free-trade interests compete to synthesize a new trade policy. Protectionist lobbying by U.S. manufacturers diminishes as labor union pressures increase. Seeking new allies to replace once-protectionist industrialists, labor organizations associate themselves with environmentalists. Meanwhile, some U.S. manufacturers profess to find new forms of unfair activities among their competitors abroad as do agricultural interests. In Mexico, policy innovations and new interindustry and intergroup conflicts materialize.

As a result of these conflicting and ever-changing pressures and counterpressures, NAFTA liberalizes trade on some fronts, particularly in services, and increases protection on others, as in the rules for domestic/North American content in automobiles and textiles. Despite these latter provisions and reservations in NAFTA, the agreements on the whole provide important opportunities to increase trade in North America, to signal the continuing U.S. commitment to

---

[14]   Baer, "New Patterns of Conflict and Cooperation," in M.D. Baer & S. Weintraub (eds.), *The NAFTA Debate: Grappling with Unconventional Trade Issues* 185-186 (1994). See also in the same volume the chapter by Wiarda, "The U.S. Domestic Politics of the U.S.-Mexico Free Trade Agreement," *id.* at 117-144.

free trade in general, and to free trade in particular with respect to trade in services, to intellectual property rights protection, and trade-related aspects of foreign investment.

Such economic integration as occurs in NAFTA, however, may be seen as a side effect of a trade policy dialectic that continues. NAFTA expands freer trade in North America, but the Clinton administration also entered simultaneously into new agreements with Mexico to restrict and cushion the effects of trade openings in some types of agricultural trade, including sugar and fruit juice. Meanwhile, as NAFTA encourages trade, NAFTA-related side agreements[15] at the same time open broader opportunities for protectionists to reduce trade through appeals against environmental and workplace enforcement in areas with only little direct effect on the international exchange of goods and services.[16] NAFTA opens trade, but the dialectic moves onward.

Renowned international economist Jagdish Bhagwati has put this apparent contradiction into sharper focus:

> This [U.S.] obsession with free trade areas strikes a blow at the multilateral trading system in ways that are either ill-understood or deliberately discounted, disregarded and distorted by politicians and lobbyists. Free trade areas -- even though sanctioned by the GATT and now the World Trade Organization -- are altogether different from multilaterally negotiated trade liberalization. They are two-faced, bringing free trade to members, but amounting to implied protection against non-members. It is Orwellian newspeak to call these free trade areas.[17]

Finally, the dialectic process of U.S. trade policy exposes the tenuous assumption of the Bush and later Clinton administrations that the pursuit of free trade areas such as NAFTA have a benign effect on multilateral trade negotiations. As Bhagwati notes,

> As such areas proliferate, trade policy links among countries become increasingly tangled, like spaghetti in a bowl. Discrimination clutters trade, with inevitable costs. Inherently arbitrary rules of origin, for example, must be devised. When is a Honda made in Canada of imported components Canadian, not Japanese, and hence eligible for free entry into the U.S.? Even when arbitrary rules are agreed, legal disputes,

---

[15] *Cf.* U.S. Trade Rep., *The NAFTA: Supplemental Agreements* (Sept. 13, 1993); *id., The NAFTA: Report on Environmental Issues* (Nov. 1993).

[16] For example, for an analysis of how "environmental demands became part of the mix of questions to be dealt with in what originally was to be purely a trade agreement," see Fox, "Environment and Trade: The NAFTA Case," 110 *Pol. Sci. Q.* 49-68 (Spring 1995).

[17] Bhagwati, "The high cost of free trade areas," *Financial Times (London)*, May 31, 1995, at 13.

corruption of officials, and the co-opting of both rules and officials by protectionists will follow.[18]

3. NAFTA: INTERNATIONAL NEGOTIATIONS AND TWO-LEVEL GAMES

A second perspective on NAFTA attempts to go beyond the observation that domestic factors influence international affairs and vice-versa, as well as the dialectical nature of United States trade policy, to seek theories that integrate both the domestic and international spheres, accounting for the areas of entanglement between them. This analytical approach builds on two premises. The first is the anecdotal observation of former U.S. trade negotiator, Robert Strauss, about his experience in the GATT negotiations: "During my tenure as Special Trade Representative, I spent as much time negotiating with domestic constituents (both industry and labor) and members of the U.S. Congress as I did negotiating with our foreign trading partners."[19] Economist Paul Krugman has articulated the second premise: "For the United States, NAFTA is essentially a foreign-policy rather than an economic issue."[20]

Therefore, one can usefully conceptualize the politics of international negotiations, especially international trade negotiations such as NAFTA, as a two-level game.[21] At the national level, domestic interest groups pursue their concerns by lobbying the government to produce favorable policies, and politicians respond by constructing coalitions among these groups in order to seek influence and power. At the international level, national governments seek to maximize their own possibilities for satisfying domestic interests, while simultaneously minimizing the adverse consequences of foreign affairs and other nations' policies to the national interest. National leaders cannot afford to neglect either game, guarding the sovereignty of their own state while acknowledging the constraints of interdependence with other nations.

> Each national political leader appears at both game boards. Across the international table sit his foreign counterparts, and at his elbows sit diplomats and other international advisers. Around the domestic table behind him sit party and parliamentary figures, spokesmen for domestic agencies, representatives of key interest groups, and

---

[18]   *Id.*
[19]   Robert S. Strauss, "Foreword" to J. E. Twiggs, *The Tokyo Round of Multilateral Trade Negotiations: A Case Study in Building Domestic Support for Diplomacy* vii (1987).
[20]   Krugman, *supra* note 1, at 13-19.
[21]   *See* Putnam, "Diplomacy and Domestic Politics: The Logic of Two-Level Games," 42 *Int'l Org.* 427-460 (Summer 1988).

the leader's own political advisers. The unusual complexity of this two-level game is that moves that are rational for a player at one board (such as raising energy prices, conceding territory, or limiting auto imports) may be impolitic for that same player at the other board. Nevertheless, there are powerful incentives for consistency between the two games.[22]

The political possibilities and complexities for the "players" in this two-level game are astounding. Any key participant at the international table who does not like the outcome may turn over the game board; and conversely, any leader who fails to satisfy his fellow players at the domestic table risks being thrown out of his seat (i.e., not re-elected). Clever players may, however, on occasion identify a move on one game board which will spur realignments on the other board (or boards), empowering this player to realize otherwise unattainable objectives. This "two-table" metaphor and approach consequently better captures the dynamics of international trade negotiations and processes such as NAFTA than any analytical model based on unitary national actors. This perspective presents a framework for examining and considering the combined, simultaneous impact of domestic and international factors on international bargaining. (See Figure 1.)

The two-level-games approach is based on the assumption that statesmen attempt typically to accomplish two objectives at once, that is, they seek to manipulate politics and reach agreement on the two levels--domestic and international--simultaneously. According to Putnam, a set of intertwined domestic and international negotiations exists in which it is impossible to reach agreement in the international negotiation without creating some kind of overlapping "win-sets"--sets of all possible international arrangements that are acceptable to the domestic constituents of both sides. Stated differently, "Diplomatic strategies and tactics are constrained both by what other states will accept and by what domestic constituencies will ratify. Diplomacy is a process of strategic interaction in which actors simultaneously try to take account of and, if possible, influence the expected reactions of other actors, both at home and abroad."[23]

---

[22] *Id.* at 434.

[23] Moravcsik, "Introduction: Integrating International and Domestic Theories of International Bargaining," in P.B. Evans, H.K. Jacobson, & R.D. Putnam (eds.), *Double-Edged Diplomacy: International Bargaining and Domestic Politics* 15 (1993)

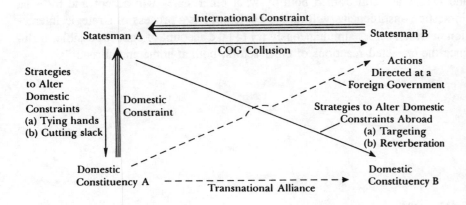

SOURCE: Andrew Moravcsik, "Introduction: Integrating International and Domestic Theories of International Bargaining," in Peter B. Evans, Harold K. Jacobson, and Robert D. Putnam (eds.), *Double-Edged Diplomacy: International Bargaining and Domestic Politics* (Berkeley: University of California Press, 1993), pp. 31-34.

This perspective counters the notion inherent in the dialectical framework above that the strong but contradicting societal inputs constrain the choices that a government like that of the United States can make in international trade bargaining, forcing it to maintain a balance between the conflicting goals and interests of economic nationalism and free trade. Instead, the two-level-games approach suggests that the outcome of such international negotiations may depend on the strategy that a statesman chooses to influence his own and his counterpart's domestic polities. For example, by controlling information and resources, utilizing agenda-setting tactics, and making side payments with regard to his own domestic constituency, the statesman can reveal or expand new possibilities for international agreement or bargaining advantage. Conversely, the statesman may employ various strategies internationally to influence the balance of interests and support domestically. Putnam notes that "economic interdependence multiplies the opportunities for altering domestic coalitions (and thus policy outcomes) by expanding the set of feasible alternatives in this way -- in effect, creating political entanglements across national boundaries."[24] Finally, the statesman can also target policies directly at domestic groups in the foreign country, in the effort to enlist allies "behind the back" of his international counterpart. In summary, the statesman, such as the President of the United States, stands "Janus-faced" -- forced to balance both domestic and international concerns in an on-going and complex process of "double-edged" diplomacy and bargaining.[25] The perspective distinctively stresses the interaction between the two levels of the negotiating game, and that moreover the statesman may simultaneously exploit strategies and opportunities on both levels in a bargaining situation.

3.1 TWO-LEVEL GAMES AND THE NAFTA NEGOTIATIONS

The metaphor and framework of "two-level games" captures certain qualities of the international negotiations on NAFTA as well as the fact that NAFTA is a continuing process and not just a product.[26] The statesman, the President of the

---

[24] Putnam, *supra* note 21, at 448.

[25] *Cf. Double-Edged Diplomacy*, *supra* note 23. See, in particular, the contributions by Kraus, "U.S.-Japan Negotiations on Construction and Semiconductors, 1985-1988: Building Friction and Relation-Chips," *id.* at 265-300; Odell, "International Threats and Internal Politics: Brazil, the European Community, and the United States, 1985-1987," *id.* at 233-264.

[26] See, for example, this perspective applied in international debt negotiation in H.P. Lehman & J. L. McCoy, "The Dynamics of the Two-Level Bargaining Game: The Brazil-

United States (and his advisers), was strategically positioned between the NAFTA game "tables," one representing domestic politics and the other international negotiation. (In order to render the graphic depiction of the NAFTA "game" more accurately, it would be necessary to have three "tables," or two simultaneous two-level games -- a task beyond the scope of this chapter.) Diplomatic tactics and strategies in the NAFTA negotiations were constrained simultaneously by what Mexico (and Canada) would accept and what U.S. domestic constituencies would ratify. That is, in order to conclude the NAFTA negotiations successfully, the Bush administration, and subsequently the Clinton administration, had to bargain on these two tables, both reaching an international agreement and securing its domestic ratification.

On the domestic "table," the two administrations utilized the full range of classical tactics to expand the NAFTA win-set and ensure the domestic ratification: "tying hands," "cutting slack," and liberal use of side payments (see Figure 1). By employing the "fast track" procedures of the Trade Act of 1974, Presidents Bush and Clinton forced an up-or-down vote on NAFTA as a whole and removed the potential obstacles of amendment by the Congress. "Fast track" use also served to influence the international negotiations in turn, as Washington persuaded Mexico City that the United States had to have an agreement that could clear U.S. ratification successfully. On the other hand, the Clinton administration assiduously employed the "cutting slack" tactic in the conclusion of the parallel negotiations and the achievement of the side agreements on the environment, the workplace and labor standards, and on adjustment assistance and retraining. The side agreements were a necessary political complement to the "tying hands" approach, especially in ensuring sufficient support from the President's own Democratic Party colleagues in Congress. Finally, side payments took the form of special provisions in agriculture (sugar, citrus products, etc.), North American content for the automobile industry, and restrictive rules of origin for the textile and apparel sectors.

3.2 ENVIRONMENTAL BARGAINING AND SIDE AGREEMENTS

NAFTA is clearly the "greenest ever" trade agreement, one which linked two hitherto unrelated issue areas -- foreign trade and the environment.[27] The per-

---

ian Debt Negotiations," 44 *World Politics* 600-644 (July 1992); and in international trade in agriculture, W.P. Avery (ed.), *World Agriculture and the GATT* (1993).
[27] For a splendid analysis of how the two issues became "linked" in the NAFTA case, see Fox, *supra* note 16, at 49-62.

spective of "two-level games" is especially useful in assessing not only why and how the two issues became linked in NAFTA, but also the evolution of the elaborate provisions for the settlement of environmental disputes between the NAFTA parties.

The linking of trade and environmental concerns in NAFTA is also interesting in that such diplomatic linkage had traditionally been avoided by the United States, and remained conspicuously absent from the U.S.-Canada Free Trade Agreement of 1988, even though a bilateral dispute over acid rain was raging at the time of the negotiations.[28] Not coincidentally, when U.S. and Canadian representatives began negotiating with their Mexican counterparts on the complex provisions of NAFTA, the parties abandoned the customary rule against linkage. From the beginning, environmental demands became part of the mix of issues which the three countries had to acknowledge and deal with in what was thought originally to be solely a free trade agreement. From the outset, two "games" or levels of linkage developed, one involving bargaining across international borders among trade representatives and diplomats, the other focused on domestic politics. The Bush administration quickly made apparent that it had readily given in to demands to include environmental concerns in the trilateral negotiations.

The United States did not need this linkage to strengthen its position on trade, but the negotiators' position would have been somewhat weaker if there were vocal domestic opposition to the trade accord at that time. All three governments, for their own reasons, wanted a trade agreement enough to adjust to the others' sensitivities about how to reach it. They all claimed similar environmental goals, differing only on the appropriate means. Since the United States was by far the strongest trade partner and had the most aggressive and influential environmentalist groups, it did not have to make trade concessions to environmental issues considered.[29]

In effect, the United States employed "moves" on the international "table" of negotiations with Mexico, in that Mexican authorities had clearly initiated and wanted the NAFTA trade and investment provisions, to exact far-reaching commitments from Mexico on the environment. These moves, broadened and more sharply articulated by the Clinton administration, secured a broader "win-set" of agreements which could then be used to gain ratification of NAFTA in the U.S. domestic sphere through the endorsement of at least some of the many highly engaged environmentalist lobbies and their allies in the Congress. In turn, the

---

[28] *Cf.* J.J. Schott & M.G. Smith (eds.), *The Canada-United States Free Trade Agreement: The Global Impact* (1988).

[29] *Id.* at 60.

White House, with strong pressure from Vice President Al Gore and others, utilized the vocal engagement of the many U.S. environmentalist groups to per- suade the Mexican government to lean on the Mexican business sector to make regulatory and environmental commitments which the latter were not necessarily disposed to undertake. Mexico City, then, was able to assuage the country's business interests by demonstrating the prospect of more open U.S. markets and the promise of major flows of foreign direct investment and capital from the north.

Having secured the international "game," the Clinton administration then had to return to the domestic board to ensure the required Congressional approval. A somewhat different form of linkage took place on the domestic U.S. front -- tactical, a kind of logrolling -- focused on the need for consensus on the specific environmental requirements of NAFTA.[30] The stakes of these coalitional struggles, played out by pro- and anti-NAFTA environmental lobbies and diverse interests in Congress, were the legislation required to implement the main NAFTA agreement, bolstered by the supplementary accords.[31] For Presi- dent Clinton the timing and context were crucial, as the side agreements negoti- ations took place with Democrats in control of both Houses of Congress and the White House. The environmentalists had prominent friends in high places, such as Gore and Interior Secretary Bruce Babbit. With key Democratic leaders, concerned members of Congress, and environmental and labor groups all look- ing over their shoulders, the U.S. trade negotiators had to devise how many concessions to environmental demands would mollify congressional advocates sufficient for the treaty ratification, while not alienating NAFTA's chief allies in the American business community. Simultaneously, the President (and his advisers) as chief statesman had to cajole the other two governments to come around to the preferred position of the United States on environmental issues, while also attaining U.S. interests on the trade and investment fronts.

The most sensitive negotiation in this area, and the one that obviously com- bined both "games" or levels of linkage, revolved around the question of whether to have trade sanctions to ensure that all parties carried out the environ- mental terms in the agreement. On one side the environmentalists, mainly in the United States but backed by emerging groups in Mexico, clearly favored their

[30] For background, see Ward & Prichett, "Prospects for a Green Trade Agreement," 34 *Environment* 34-45 (May 1992); French, "Reconciling Trade and the Environment," in World Watch Institute, *State of the World, 1993* (1993).
[31] *Cf.* Wiarda, "The U.S. Domestic Politics of the U.S.-Mexico Free Trade Agreement," in M.D. Baer & S. Weintraub (eds.), *The NAFTA Debate: Grappling with Unconventional Trade Issues* 117-144 (1994).

traditional methods of achieving their goals through government regulation backed up by legal sanctions, including court suits. On the other side was big business in all three countries, but especially North American-based multinational corporations. The corporate view favored reliance on cooperation for compliance, with the less governmental interference the better. Likewise, both the Mexican and Canadian governments were averse to using trade penalties to enforce environmental rules.[32] The Mexicans were sensitive to issues of sovereignty; the Canadians through their long experience with the colossus to the south were concerned that, as the smaller and less powerful partner, they would be the target rather than the instigator of such sanctions.

> As a result of all these cross pressures, the ultimate compromise was the convoluted dispute settlement system. The administration in the United States stressed that the intention was to deter and correct rather than to punish.[33]

In addition, the drafting of the supplementary environment agreement was a kind of side payment for endorsing NAFTA. Such side deals, indispensable for persuading those who might otherwise lose from linking NAFTA's free trade provisions with non-trade issues, were made all during the negotiations.[34] A further accord between the United States and Mexico responded to the concerns about cleaning up the pollution along the borders between the two countries.[35] To an unprecedented degree, the USTR consulted environmental groups throughout the negotiation for NAFTA, along with congressional staffs and committees. The linkage of environment and trade on the domestic level was expedited by the lack of major bureaucratic rivalry, strong advocates in the administration, the sensitivity of many trade officials to the issues, and understated opposition. The USTR collaborated with the EPA to push the concerns forward in the Washington interagency process.

> Partly as a result of such collaboration, most of the environmentalists' demands found a response in the provisions of the NAFTA and particularly in the supplemental envi-

---

[32] *Cf.* G.C. Hufbauer & J.J. Schott, *NAFTA: An Assessment* 91-104 (rev. ed. 1993).

[33] Fox, *supra* note 16, at 62.

[34] *Cf.* U.S. Dept. of State, 4 *Dispatch* 591 (no. 34, August 23, 1993). For an analysis of the role of side payments in negotiations, see Mayer, "Managing Domestic Differences in International Negotiations: the Strategic Use of Internal Side Payments," 46 *Int'l Org.* 796-816 (Autumn 1992).

[35] *Cf.* Gilbreath & Tonra, "The Environment: Unwelcome Guest at the Free Trade Party," in M. D. Baer & S. Weintraub, *supra* note 31, at 33-93.

ronmental agreement, which made much more explicit the commitments in the principal agreement and also added to them.[36]

On the international level, the successful linking of environmental demands
with trade claims was facilitated in part by the fact that there were more than two
parties to the negotiations. Both the Mexicans and Canadians had stakes in
NAFTA too high to block the environmental issues, while claiming sympathy at
least with objectives the environmentalists were striving for.[37] Their concerns
with U.S. unilateral extraterritorial measures were assuaged by preventing the
inclusion of trade sanctions for environmental non-compliance (an international
side payment), and the fact that environmental interests in all three countries
attained the right to be heard.[38]

The Clinton administration, at the center of the "game" boards, wisely translated tactical gains won through careful maneuvering on the domestic "table"
into strategic positions on the international level which Washington sold to its
negotiating partners as cooperative and mutually beneficial. The "double" nature
of this diplomacy, however, ensures that the game continues and that NAFTA is
still an unfolding process and not a final agreement on regional economic integration.

4. NAFTA AND THE STRATEGIC POLICY OF MULTINATIONAL CORPORATIONS

A third perspective examines the strategic behavior in response to the NAFTA
accords of important actors at an analytical level below the nation-state--the
multinational corporation (MNC). MNCs have both anticipated and preceded the
potential effects of NAFTA in devising their corporate investment and production decisions in the North American market. On the other hand, MNCs will also
need to adjust their policy to the mix of NAFTA's trade liberalizing and protectionist elements (noted in the first perspective). This focus on multinational
behavior contends that economic integration has been occurring in North

---

[36] Fox, *supra* note 16, at 63.

[37] For an assessment that concludes, in line with assurances by Mexican officials, that "a
reduction in pollution may well be a side benefit of increased Mexican specialization and
trade" spurred by NAFTA, see Grossman & Kreuger, "Environmental Impacts of a North
American Free Trade Agreement," in P.M. Garber (ed.), *Mexico-U.S. Free Trade Agreement* 13-56, 48 (1993).

[38] For a somewhat skeptical view, see Shrybman, "Trading Away the Environment," in
R. Grinspun & M.A. Cameron (eds.), *The Political Economy of North American Free Trade*
271-296 (1993).

America, less through the negotiated agreements of the three partner countries than by the prior and continuing investment decisions of private business.

NAFTA has far-reaching implications for corporate decision makers in its market. NAFTA will likely enhance the private investment climate in three ways: it will open up the Mexican economy to Canadian and U.S. investors, it will provide enhanced security for all foreign direct investment (FDI) in the NAFTA area, and it intends to make more transparent the discriminatory measures that each of the three signatories have chosen to maintain.[39] Conversely, NAFTA also has many protectionist investment-related measures, particularly the rules of origin (especially as they apply to automotive and textile and apparel sectors) and the lists of exemptions from national treatment. Although MNCs will have to adjust to the changes NAFTA sets in motion, studies have found that the large MNCs have already adopted new strategies to benefit from NAFTA in advance of the treaty, also to offset any potential negative impacts. The conclusion is that for large MNCs the impact of NAFTA is likely to be neutral.[40] NAFTA therefore has only a marginal influence upon North American economic integration, but it still initiates a significant process of adjustment for these transnational actors simultaneously with trade liberalizing and protectionist trends.

4.1   MNC STRATEGIC DECISIONS AND NAFTA

Multinationals' activities clearly dominate economic relations among the three NAFTA countries. As economic and strategic actors, MNCs both respond and adjust to changes in their environment and act to shape this milieu to their advantage. Contrary to conventional economic analysis which tends to classify environmental change as exogenous to the decision-making processes of firms, MNCs are characterized by two distinct advantages. These advantages are 1) the MNC's ability to internalize portions of their value-added chains, and 2) the capacity to change the environment in which they operate. The latter advantage, resulting in NAFTA's reflection of MNC interests through their lobbying

---

[39]   *Cf.* Hufbauer & Schott, *supra* note 32, at 79-91. For a detailed analysis of the investment provisions, see Gestrin & Rugman, "The North American Free Trade Agreement and Foreign Direct Investment," 3 *Transnat'l Corp.* 77-96 (Feb. 1994).

[40]   *See* Rugman & Gestrin, "The strategic response of multinational corporations to NAFTA," 28 *Colum. J. World Bus.* 18-29 (Winter 1993); Rugman & Gestrin, "The investment provisions of NAFTA," in S. Globerman & M. Walker, *supra* note 12, at 271-292.

efforts, translates into the MNC having the ability to expand the logic of internalization to a NAFTA-wide region.

4.1.1 Internalization[41] and MNC Response to NAFTA

The multinational corporation employs a process of strategic planning in which the MNC constantly reassesses its corporate strengths in light of new information about the domestic and international environments in which it operates. Such changes include the trade liberalization and protectionist measures reflected in NAFTA. Internalization theory explains how MNCs respond to such environmental change. Through internalization, the MNC maximizes the benefits of its particular technology or production processes in a target market. These strategic benefits accrue from the combination of Firm Specific Advantages (FSAs) held by the firm and Country Specific Advantages (CSAs) characterizing the national economies in which the MNC operates.[42] "Internalization allows a multinational enterprise to establish and maintain better proprietary control over its FSAs so that the economic rents of these do not accrue to other firms."[43]

The theory of internalization further suggests that a MNC analyzes explicitly the relative costs of servicing foreign markets in one of several ways. First, the MNC may simply decide to export to foreign markets. Second, the firm may engage in foreign direct investment, that is, set up an overseas subsidiary to produce for a local market. Third, the firm may conclude that the best strategy may change over time; new activities by firms abroad typically follow these three stages: 1) exporting; 2) FDI; and 3) licensing. The application of internalization theory to NAFTA is instructive:

> Due to its institutional complexity, and the balancing of trade liberalization with protectionist measures, it is highly unlikely that under NAFTA the current business practices of MNEs [MNCs] already active in North America will be altered in any significant manner. Even before NAFTA, most MNEs had already organized their activities

---

[41] For a detailed discussion of the theory of internalization, see Rugman, "A New Theory of the Multinational Enterprise: Internationalization Versus Internalization," 15 *Colum. J. World Bus.* 23-29 (Spring 1980).

[42] FSAs are defined as the competitive strengths of the company. These can be either production-based (cost or innovation advantages) or marketing-based (customization advantages). CSAs at basis are defined as the natural factor endowments of a nation, but these CSAs can be influenced, even changed, by government policies. *Id.* For a detailed analysis of MNC strategic decision-making and internalization theory, see A.M. Rugman, *Inside the Multinationals: The Economics of Internal Markets* (1981).

[43] Rugman & Gestrin, "The strategic response of multinational corporations to NAFTA," *supra* note 40, at 20.

across the three national borders to take advantage of relative factor costs and to prevent dissipation of their firm-specific advantages....The NAFTA reflects the agenda of the MNEs and it will not remove the rationale for internalization.[44]

In short, the trade measures and institutional provisions of NAFTA will reinforce but not substantially accelerate or change the degree of transborder economic integration well underway in North America. Only a future deepening of NAFTA and the achievement of full and unambiguous "free trade" would serve to eliminate the need for MNC strategies geared to FDI and/or licensing and allow MNCs to concentrate on exporting alone.

4.1.2 Operations as Usual

Studies of the multinationals' response in anticipation of the U.S.-Canada Free Trade Agreement which went into effect in 1988, and their subsequent adjustment to the actual impact of the FTA, further suggest that MNCs have calculated the likelihood of NAFTA coming into effect and incorporated those judgements into their strategic planning well before 1994. Here it is important to note as well that Mexico began the unilateral liberalization of its economy starting in the mid-1980s, and that the U.S.-Canada investment relationship, the largest in the world between two countries, had assimilated the terms of the FTA at least six years before NAFTA. This is to say that NAFTA, then, from the perspective of the largest MNCs is a reflection and continuation of North American economic relationships marked by trends toward economic liberalization well underway over the past decade. These relationships have been shaped and driven by the strategic activities of the MNCs.[45]

Therefore, MNCs are not primarily reactive actors to the political and legislative implications of NAFTA's ratification. They have been predicating their strategies on the underlying forces and processes of economic change in force now for over a decade in North America.[46] In effect, these very fundamental changes themselves ultimately have made NAFTA politically viable in all three countries. A focus on the MNCs consequently finds NAFTA having little direct impact upon the signatories' economies, with most of the change taking place in

---

[44] *Id.* at 21.

[45] *Cf.* Graham & Wilkie, "Multinationals and the investment provisions of the NAFTA," 8 *Int'l Trade J.* 9-38 (Spring 1994).

[46] *Cf.* Weintraub, "Modeling the Industrial Effects of NAFTA," in Lustig *et al.*, *supra* note 3, at 109-143.

Mexico due to some trade and investment diversion to that country from other developing states.

> Previous experience in the case of the [U.S.-Canada] FTA provides support for the view that most MNEs are motivated by a complex "basket" of factors such that the mild (and gradual) liberalization measures of agreements like the FTA and the NAFTA are not sufficient to warrant large scale organizational readjustments.[47]

4.2   NAFTA AND MNC COMPETITIVE ADVANTAGE

At this point, it may be useful to look at the potential effects of NAFTA upon the competitive positions of MNCs operating in the North American market. Analytically, it is possible to assess whether or not an industry benefits from strong CSAs (competitive position within its national market), and whether or not the industry itself possesses strong or weak FSAs (competitive strength of the company). For this purpose, CSAs and FSAs are both defined as an advantage sufficient to ensure competitiveness with respect to foreign rivals. A typology of MNC competitiveness therefore emerges.[48] (See Figure 2).

Figure 2 presents a means of classifying the competitive position of industries in terms of their respective FSAs and CSAs. International competitiveness is assured whenever an industry's FSAs and CSAs are both strong (quadrant 1). If an industry's position in terms of the home market (CSAs: resource endowments and impact of government policies) is weak, it will need to have a strong internal competitive position (FSAs) to compensate (quadrant 2). Likewise, strong CSAs may overcome the disadvantages of weak FSAs (quadrant 3). Finally, industries with simultaneously weak CSAs and FSAs (quadrant 4) will find competing with efficient foreign rivals virtually impossible. Industries (and firms) finding themselves in the position of quadrant 4, or moving that way because of the effects of economic and political change, such as that catalyzed by the formation of NAFTA, will experience the greatest effects of NAFTA liberalization. It is possible to infer from this typology that industries which have already adapted to an increasingly open and integrated North American market, i.e., those which have

---

[47]   Rugman & Gestrin, "The strategic response of multinational corporations to NAFTA," *supra* note 40, at 22.

[48]   For a detailed discussion of CSA and FSA sufficiency and the generic competitive advantage matrix, see A.M. Rugman & A. Verbeke, *Global Corporate Strategy and Trade Policy* (1990) (especially ch. 30). Rugman and Verbeke build upon Michael Porter's concept of the "diamond" of international competitiveness. *See* Porter, *The Competitive Advantage of Nations* (1990); Rugman & Verbeke, "How to Operationalize Porter's Diamond of International Competitiveness," 33 *Int'l Executive* 283-299 (July/Aug. 1993).

internalized their production, will continue to push for liberalization. Industries and MNCs which have previously adjusted to the market and internalized their production across the three NAFTA country markets will likely seek protectionism through NAFTA or be hard pressed to survive renewed international competitive pressures. Such protectionism will take the form of attempting to strengthen their CSAs through treaty provisions and governmental policy with respect to competitors in other NAFTA markets.

Figure 2 - The Competitive Advantage Matrix

Firm Specific Advantages

		Strong	Weak
Country and Region Specific Advantages	Strong	1 Both FSAs and CSAs/RSAs are strong. International competitiveness is assured.	3 FSAs are weak. Strong CSAs and RSAs are therefore necessary to maintain an internationally competitive position.
	Weak	2 CSAs and RSAs are weak. FSAs are required for industry to compete with global rivals.	4 Both FSAs and CSAs are weak. Competing internationally with foreign rivals is impossible.

SOURCE: Adapted from Alan M. Rugman and Alain Verbeke, *Global Corporate Strategy and Trade Policy* (New York: Routledge, 1990), Chapter 3.

4.3   NAFTA'S POSSIBLE IMPACT ON INDUSTRIES' NATIONAL COMPETITIVENESS

One can then proceed to utilize the competitive advantage matrix to assess the probable effect of NAFTA on selected industries.[49] Figure 3 is therefore concerned only with those selected industries from the three NAFTA countries likely to experience change under NAFTA, that is, a strengthening or weakening of their respective CSAs or FSAs. (See Figure 3).

---

[49]   Positions have been categorized on the basis of a number of detailed studies. U.S. Int'l Trade Comm., Potential Impact on the U.S. Economy and Selected Industries of the North American Free Trade Agreement (1993, publication 2596); G.C. Hufbauer & J.J. Schott, *supra* note 32 (especially ch. 3); A.R. Riggs & T. Velk (eds.), *Beyond NAFTA: An Economic, Political and Sociological Perspective* (1993); Competitiveness Policy Council, Annual Report to the President and the Congress: Building a Competitive America (March 1993).

Figure 3 - The Impact of NAFTA upon Country Specific Advantages

Firm Specific Advantages

		Strong	Weak
Country Specific Advantages	**Strengthened by NAFTA**	1 **United States** High technology related to defense; some energy. **Canada** Some energy. **Mexico** None.	3 **United States** Maritime; cabotage; steel; agriculture; textiles. **Canada** Culture; agriculture. **Mexico** Energy; telecom. services; natural resources.
	Weakened by NAFTA	2 **United States** None. **Canada** Apparel. **Mexico** None.	4 **United States** Apparel; citrus products; roses; household applicances. **Canada** Textiles; household appliances; steel; beer. **Mexico** Most manufacturing.

SOURCE: Adapted from Alan M. Rugman and Michael Gestrin, "The strategic response of multinational corporations to NAFTA," *Columbia Journal of World Business* 28, No. 4 (Winter 1993), pp. 23-28.

Quadrant 1 primarily concerns industries or sectors accorded "artificial" CSAs (those generated by government), those examples where governments have targeted sectors for special advantage or protection even though these industries' own internal competitiveness would not warrant this consideration. U.S. high technology industries related to defense are so designated as well as certain Canadian energy sectors (such as uranium). Quadrant 3 is more interesting in that it contains the industries that are conventionally known as the "sacred cows" of each of the NAFTA partners. Competitively weak internally, these industries or sectors have acquired strong leverage or political clout in their respective domestic contexts. As noted earlier in this chapter, the U.S. "sacred cows" are little affected by NAFTA; especially the maritime sector, transportation, steel, and many agricultural products received particular protection under the terms of NAFTA. Likewise in Canada, the best example is the cultural sector. Mexico's chief "sacred cows" are the energy sector (coal being one of the few areas liberalized), telecommunications services, and control over natural resources. These areas with weak FSAs but receiving protection under NAFTA did so under Mexico's Annex 3 Constitutional reservations.[50]

Quadrant 2 is notably empty reflecting "the fact that the NAFTA, on the whole, has not made North America a more dynamic and competitive environment for firms that already enjoy strong FSAs." The main exception, Canadian apparel, is due to the fact that considerable tightening of the NAFTA content rules for textiles and apparel will make it very difficult for the formerly highly competitive Canadian industry to source high quality, inexpensive textiles outside the NAFTA community as the bases for its products.

Predictably, quadrant 4 comprises those industries and sectors likely to experience the most significant change as a result of NAFTA. Although a number of U.S. and Canadian interests will be affected, the most striking assessment of this matrix is that quadrant 4 includes the entire Mexican manufacturing sector.[51] Following decades of import substitution policies and protectionism, Mexican industry as a whole faces fierce external competition from a position characterized by very weak FSAs. NAFTA will remove most of the manufacturing sector's protection over the 10-15 year phase-in period, although most tariff walls will disappear during the first five years of the agreement. Clearly, in comparison to the United States and Canada, Mexico will bear the brunt of NAFTA's adjustment costs. Even though Mexico has undergone a decade of economic restructuring and liberalization,[52] at a pace of economic reform seldom seen elsewhere, the challenge to its entire industrial sector sharpens the contrast to the United States and Canada where the impact of adjustment is concentrated principally on their respective sunset industries.

4.4   NAFTA'S IMPACT ON REGION SPECIFIC ADVANTAGE

A further analytical step allows the depiction of region specific advantage (RSAs) by industries, and an assessment of whether NAFTA strengthens or weakens these positions. Figure 4 examines whether or not RSAs and FSAs are

---

[50]   *Cf.* "NAFTA 'Lowlights'," in G.C. Hufbauer & J.J. Schott, *supra* note 32, at 5-7; Gestrin & Rugman, "The NAFTA's Impact on the North American Investment Regime," in C.D. Howe Inst., *Commentary* (Mar. 1993).

[51]   *Cf.* Weintraub, *supra* note 46; Juraidini, "NAFTA's Effects: A Mexican Analysis," in A.R. Riggs & Velk (eds.), *Beyond NAFTA: An Economic, Political and Sociological Perspective* 129-189 (1994); Hellman, "Mexican Perceptions of Free Trade: Support and Opposition to NAFTA," in R. Grinspun & M.A. Cameron (eds.), *The Political Economy of North American Free Trade* 193-204 (1993).

[52]   *Cf.* Arregui, "Industrial Restructuring in Mexico During the 1960s," in R. Grinspun & M.A. Cameron (eds.), *supra* note 51, at 163-176.

Louis L. Ortmayer

likely to change under NAFTA. (See Figure 4). The main difference between industries and sectors placed in this matrix compared to Figure 3 is that those in Figure 4 are characterized by industries which have already adopted a regional outlook, rather than relying essentially on national corporate structures (industries depicted in Figure 3). Industries in Figure 4 also operate on the basis of a North American border in their strategic planning and largely ignore the national boundaries separating the three NAFTA countries.

Figure 4 - The Impact of NAFTA upon Region Specific Advantages

Firm Specific Advantages

	Strong	Weak
Region Specific Advantages — Strengthened by NAFTA	1 **United States** Chemicals; computers; trucking; energy; petrochemicals; agriculture; electronics. **Canada** Chemicals; energy; some forest products. **Mexico** Electronics; apparel.	3 **United States** Autos; auto parts. **Canada** Autos; auto parts. **Mexico** TV tubes.
Weakened by NAFTA	2 **United States** None. **Canada** None. **Mexico** None.	4 **United States** None. **Canada** None. **Mexico** None.

SOURCE: Adapted from Alan M. Rugman and Michael Gestrin, "The strategic response of multinational corporations to NAFTA," *Columbia Journal of World Business* 28, No. 4 (Winter 1993), pp. 23-28.

The interpretation of Figure 4 follows similar lines to that of Figure 3. Quadrants 1-3 are largely neutral in terms of their implications for MNC investment patterns, while Quadrant 4 denotes that a profound readjustment for the sectors listed is essential. The major difference is that the investment flows highlighted in Figure 4 are those between the NAFTA region and the rest of the world.

A primary feature of Figure 4 is the fact that Quadrants 2 and 4, representing weak NAFTA-based regional competitive advantages, are empty. This assessment reflects a significant feature of MNC behavior -- "international production by large MNCs is undergoing a process of regionalization along triad lines, not a process of globalization."[53] Global production trends would regard RSAs as essentially a hindrance to lowering transaction costs for the MNCs between their NAFTA-located and non-NAFTA-based operations. With regard to NAFTA, no industries in this manner have sought to eliminate or even phase out their NAFTA-based RSAs, either in the main text of the treaties or in the lists of reservations. Consequently, if economic integration is occurring, according to this perspective it is the regional integration at the expense of global economic liberalization.

Quadrant 1 industries benefit from both strong RSAs and strong FSAs, and in contrast to their counterparts in Quadrant 1 of Figure 3, these are much more "mainstream" industries in composition. That is, sectors related to national security and attendant political protection dominated Quadrant 1, Figure 3. What NAFTA offers to industries enjoying strong RSAs is better access to a larger marketplace of productive resources (labor, infrastructure, FDI, etc.), compared to their non-NAFTA competitors. Quadrant 1, therefore, indicates that a fairly extensive list of United States industries stands to gain stronger RSAs versus their international rivals through an opening of their counterpart sectors in the Mexican market. Although some Mexican sectors will, in turn, gain stronger RSAs, the Mexican list is considerably more restricted.

4.5   NAFTA's IMPACT ON SPECIFIC INDUSTRIES: APPAREL, ELECTRONICS, AND AUTOS[54]

As a closer scrutiny of Figures 2 through 4 demonstrates, industries that merit particular attention under NAFTA are electronics and apparel (where Mexico should gain advantage) and automobiles which are a special case.[55]

In the electronics sector, NAFTA creates rules which treat this industry as if North America were already a unified and integrated market. Previously, Mexican television manufacturers could import components such as tubes duty-free for production of televisions which they could subsequently export to the United States at preferential rates. After NAFTA, there will be a tariff of 15 per-

---

[53]   Rugman & Gestrin, "The strategic response of multinational corporations to NAFTA," *supra* note 40, at 26.

[54]   For detailed analysis of these industries, see U.S. Int'l Trade Comm., Potential Impact on the U.S. Economy and Selected Industries of the North American Free Trade Agreement, pub. 2596 (1993).

[55]   Schott and Hufbauer also provide illuminating analyses of the automobile and textile and apparel sectors. *See supra* note 32, at 37-46.

cent applied to imported tubes, thereby giving significant advantage to tubes produced in the NAFTA region, where Mexico's low labor costs provide a competitive edge. Only televisions, for example, with regionally produced tubes will be allowed duty-free access into the United States, all others also facing a 5 percent tariff. In effect, NAFTA's restrictive rules of origin have granted the industry protection on a regional, not a national basis.

A similar situation exists in the apparel industry. NAFTA will reduce barriers to trade among the NAFTA countries in apparel products. Mexico, especially, will no longer be subject to the Multi-Fibre Agreement (MFA) quotas which have restricted their access in the past into the U.S. market. Extremely tight rules of origin, however, in this sector show that the apparent trade liberalization of NAFTA in this sector is undergirded by much tighter protection now granted on a regional basis. Regional integration will therefore likely accelerate in both the apparel industry and the electronics sector.[56] But this economic integration comes at the expense of wider global integration and the costs of probable diversion.

The most economically powerful industry which stands to benefit from NAFTA's impact on RSAs is the automotive industry.[57] This industry is found in Quadrant 3 of Figure 3. Relative to its Japanese and European rivals, this sector in North America suffers from weak FSAs, although the U.S. Big Three have been making major improvements in this realm since the mid-1980s. NAFTA will compensate the traditionally weak FSAs with stronger RSAs. This change is due to much tightened rules of origin (a 62.5 percent regional value content requirement is mandated for automobiles, light trucks, and their engines and transmissions), the introduction of a protectionist "tracing" formula to determine value added, and explicit distinctions between existing producers and new entrants for purposes of granting preferences to the former.[58] As with the electronics and apparel industries, the rules of origin restrictions are decidedly intended to encourage more regional production at the expense of non-NAFTA producers.

---

[56] *Cf.* Dunn, "Winners and Losers from NAFTA," in Riggs & Velk, *supra* note 51, at 89-96; Watson, "The Economics of NAFTA: How much Zero-Sum?," in *id.*, *supra* note 51, at 159-168.

[57] *Cf.* Eden & Molot, "Continentalizing the North American Auto Industry," in R. Grinspun & M.A. Cameron, *supra* note 51, at 297-314: Berry, Grilli, & de Silanes, "The Automobile Industry and the Mexico-U.S. Free Trade Agreement," in P.M. Garber (ed.), *The Mexico-U.S. Free Trade Agreement* 219-277 (1994).

[58] *Cf.* U.S. Chamber of Commerce, A Guide to the North American Free Trade Agreement: What It Means for U.S. Business (1992); Dorsey, Estimating the Restrictive Effect of FTA Rules of Origin (Office of Management and Budget, 1992)(unpublished manuscript).

As a consequence of NAFTA, within 10 years an integrated auto market will exist in North America. By world standards, the regional industry should be highly competitive. In fact, drawing on economies of scale and a variety of labor skills, North America could become the world's low-cost producer of autos and trucks, and a major net exporter of these products.[59]

4.6　NAFTA, COMPETITIVENESS, AND INTEGRATION

This examination of the relationship between MNCs and the institutional environment in which they operate provides a particular perspective on NAFTA and the process of economic integration. The application of internalization theory and the extension of the analysis of national competitive advantage to a NAFTA or regional level together argue that the impact of NAFTA upon MNC investment patterns in the United States and Canada will be minimal or largely neutral. Mexico will benefit from significant investment (and eventually trade) diversion away from other developing countries not part of NAFTA.

> By eliminating the majority of Mexico's administrative CSAs, thereby integrating the Mexican, U.S. and Canadian economies, the NAFTA has moved the North American market in a global direction. By establishing a new and expansive level of protectionism in the form of RSAs, the NAFTA reminds us that globalization is not yet a reality....[T]he agreement suggests that regionalism, and globalism, is the relevant benchmark for corporate strategy.[60]

Once again, this corporate strategy-based analytical perspective shows the paradoxical nature of NAFTA, in its propensity to apply simultaneously liberalizing and discriminatory measures to the same industry. This paradox is partly explained by the introduction of a new "administrative" level to the North American trade and investment regime. Although corporate decision makers will have to be aware of the new "playing fields" which NAFTA creates, those MNCs already engaged in internalized production decisions will continue their internationalizing begun prior to NAFTA. As Lorainne Eden has argued for the important auto industry:

> The auto industry is clearly the most integrated North American industry. [MNC] rationalization of production on a continent-wide basis, which has resulted in massive new investments in assembly and supplier capacity in both Mexico and the United

---

[59]　G.C. Hufbauer & J.J. Schott, *supra* note 32, at 43.
[60]　Rugman & Gestrin, "The strategic response of multinational corporations to NAFTA," *supra* note 40, at 28.

States, has been promoted both by state policies and the lean production technologies.
Integration in the auto industry will continue regardless of NAFTA.[61]

In summary, NAFTA will promote a more competitive, highly integrated
North American market, but at the same time it promotes regionalism over the
arguably broader economic benefits of globalization.

5. IN PLACE OF CONCLUSION

This chapter provides three perspectives in arguing that NAFTA is not a
straightforward example of economic integration but rather a complex combination of both trade liberalizing and protectionist elements. NAFTA is also a complicated amalgam of policy and process. It is not a set of agreements carved in
stone; it is a process continuously unfolding and a set of policies in becoming.

The approach to NAFTA as a variation of the dialectic captures both dimensions of the process and policy dichotomy. NAFTA viewed as a stage of the
evolutionary development of postwar U.S. international economic and trade
policy underscores the process of contention between the forces of trade liberalization and the forces of protectionism shaping U.S. relations with the world.
NAFTA, then, is a temporary synthesis produced by the compromises struck by
the contending camps, one which will be challenged continuously by the underlying economic dynamics pushing toward the globalization of production and by
the groups rallying to protect their interests against the impact of this change. In
addition, the dialectical approach illuminates NAFTA as U.S. policy, that is
complex, messy, an untidy composite of multifaceted interests, at once liberalizing and protectionist.

On a somewhat more concrete level, the concept of two-level games and of
the logic of diplomatic game outcomes contributes to an understanding of
NAFTA as the result of a complex bargaining process. Two-level-games analysis complements the notion of the dialectic in the former's emphasis not just on
the tension between free trade and protectionist interests, but also on the intricate
interaction between domestic and international politics and the chief decision-
maker's attempts to reconcile the two. The negotiation of NAFTA and the conse-
quent application of side payments, parallel negotiations, "fast-track" procedures, and special treaty provisions fit well into the two-level-games framework. Two-level-games analysis serves effectively to depict NAFTA as the elaborate consequence constituencies would ratify. This interpretation helps clarify

---

[61]   Eden & Molot, *supra* note 57, at 308.

NAFTA again as both process and policy. As process, two-level games are ongoing, just as NAFTA's unfolding record on environmental compliance, dispute settlement, and enforcement procedures, such as those for the rules of origin provisions, predicate. As policy, two-level-games theory demonstrates that the product as well as the process is dynamic, constantly changing and evolving and subject to assessment at both the interstate level and the domestic level.

Finally, the even more specific perspective of looking at NAFTA through the lens of multinational corporate strategy and through the application of internalization theory defines a NAFTA that has only marginal impact on economic trends already underway in North America, but a NAFTA that has divergent and significant impact on selected industries and economic sectors. Such a framework exposes both the liberalizing and protectionist dimensions of NAFTA, but then it further segments this dichotomy by profiling selected industries which face profoundly differing implications of NAFTA for their respective future competitive positions in a growing North American market. The most interesting finding of this approach is that NAFTA denotes economic integration on a regional level, but that NAFTA simultaneously may hinder the moves toward global integration.

In conclusion, this last assertion is important in the light of two concerns that NAFTA's creation raises. The first is that articulated by Jagdish Bhagwati and others that NAFTA is problematic for the maintenance of the postwar multilateral trade regime and international economic system.

> The U.S., long aware of the shortcomings of free trade areas, shifted course mainly because it failed to get a commitment to starting multilateral trade negotiations in 1982. Thereupon it turned to free trade areas, as the best available way to liberalize trade and jump-start multilateral trade negotiations.
>
> This strategy succeeded. Now, however, with WTO in place, multilateralism need no longer be discarded as unworkable.[62]

The second apprehension pertains to the question whether NAFTA will provide the springboard to wider economic integration, including a possible Western Hemisphere Free Trade Agreement (WHFTA). The Summit of the Americas in December 1994 called for and set plans in motion for such an agenda.[63] The Mexican peso crisis has temporarily left WHFTA in doubt. The United States government has indicated that this agenda is important:

---

[62] Bhagwati, *supra* note 17.
[63] *Cf.* Peterson, "Mad and Glad Over NAFTA," Los Angeles Times, Dec. 8, 1994, at A1, A14-15.

The dream of Western Hemisphere integration…is alive and well, despite reservations voiced in the wake of the Mexico peso crisis. For the first time in history there exists a convergence of mutual trade interests and democratic values that unites every country in the hemisphere, except Cuba.…Commercial integration among other countries of the hemisphere is moving ahead quickly. In short, the game is on, and we must compete.[64]

---

[64] McLarty, "Hemispheric Free Trade is Still a National Priority," Wall St. J., May 26, 1995, at A11. Thomas F. McLarty is Counselor to the President and Special Representative of the President and the Secretary of State for the Summit of the America

Chapter Two

MEXICO: OPEN ECONOMY, CLOSED OPTIONS
The Making of a Vulnerable Economy

by Alejandro Nadal

1. INTRODUCTION

Twelve years ago a new economic strategy was inaugurated in Mexico. It was based on the premise that opening and deregulating the economy, as well as reducing state intervention, would bring Mexico out of the economic crisis which had been brewing since the late 1970s. The central idea was that market forces, if left to themselves, would allocate resources efficiently and bring about the required growth rates that Mexico needs. The new model was designed to replace the aging and exhausted import substitution strategy pursued during the previous forty years.

Opening the economy, maintaining a fixed parity of the peso against the dollar as part of a plan to fight inflation, high real interest rates to attract foreign financial resources (and prevent capital flight) were part and parcel of the strategy implemented since 1988. The result was an enormous current account deficit which, by 1993, was being financed primarily by short-term portfolio investment. In December 1994 the situation became untenable and an unprecedented economic crisis was triggered by the devaluation of the Mexican peso.

The crisis came as a surprise to many, although several alarming signs had been identified since 1990. Unemployment rates (open and disguised), social indicators, income maldistribution, evolution of domestic industrial production, and, of course, the increasing current account deficit, already were disturbing signs back in 1991-92. However, a combination of events helped conceal this:

35

D. G. Dallmeyer (ed.), Joining Together, Standing Apart: National Identities after NAFTA, 35–62.
© 1997 Kluwer Law International. Printed in the Netherlands.

the conclusion of the renegotiation of the external debt (carried out between 1988-1990), the massive privatization program involving more than US$20.5 billion, a frantic effort to deregulate the economy, and finally the injection of fresh credit by monetary authorities which allowed for a downward trend in the rate of interest were among the factors supporting moderate rates of growth of gross domestic product (GDP). In addition, the manipulation of data, control of the media, and the frantic lobbying that took place during the negotiations to approve the North American Free Trade Agreement (NAFTA) by the U.S. Congress, kept the public largely misinformed about the realities of the Mexican economy. The fabrication of an image of success for the Mexican economy reached its pinnacle with the admission of Mexico as a full-fledged member of the Organization for Economic Cooperation and Development (OECD).

The crisis revealed the vulnerability of the economic achievements of the previous government. It also helped reveal the truth behind the economic indicators of the past twelve years. Behind the glitter of official propaganda, the economy as a whole had a mediocre performance over this period, not only in terms of growth, but also in terms of the external accounts. It was also quite unsatisfactory in terms of the evolution of real incomes of workers and from the viewpoint of the proportion of the Mexican population living below the poverty line. Finally, almost all inequality indicators had worsened, and the economy had become more vulnerable.

To make matters worse, the crisis was confronted by an unimaginative government whose only recipe is a contractionist policy package which is taking the economy into the worst recession in recent economic history. This policy package is not designed to solve the roots of the external disequilibrium, and will only help meet short-term financial commitments. In the process, it will dismantle a significant portion of Mexico's productive capacity. As a direct result of these policies, thousands of firms have closed their operations and many more have opened bankruptcy procedures during the first half of 1995. Hundreds of thousands of employees have been ousted, doubling open unemployment in six months. Inflation will reach 50 percent this year. The non-performing portfolio of the private banking system has grown by more than 300 percent and the external debt burden has become intolerably heavy.

This chapter examines the vulnerability of the economic model pursued by Mexican authorities since 1984. In the first section we present a short review of the initial process by which the old protectionist strategy was dismantled (1982-1988). The second section examines the alleged successes of the Salinas administration: this section focuses on the struggle against inflation, reduction of the fiscal deficit, privatization, and NAFTA. The scrutiny of performance in these areas is presented in the third section, covering the evolution of the current account deficit, the external debt problem, unemployment, income maldistribution, and social expenditure. Also examined here is the critical question of whether Mexico's economy is evolving into an export-led growth economy. A fourth section is centered on the response of the Zedillo administration to the economic crisis. The final remarks are directed towards the prospects for the Mexican economy in the coming months.

2. DISMANTLING PROTECTIONISM: 1982-1988

As the presidential campaign of 1982 approached in Mexico the current account balance deteriorated dramatically. The high rate of indebtedness incurred under the López Portillo administration in order to consolidate Mexico's oil and petrochemical exporting capacity boomeranged as interest rates went upwards and oil prices declined.

The presidential elections took place in July 1982. As the Partido Revolucionario Institucional (PRI) candidate, Miguel de la Madrid, campaigned throughout Mexico for ten months before the elections, no mention was made of the impending financial crisis. Only a small circle of officials and academics knew that Mexico's international reserves would not hold until the end of 1982: a large proportion of that debt was reaching maturity in the short term. A desperate last-minute attempt to reschedule the debt failed early in the summer of that year, and it became clear that a unilateral moratorium would have to be declared.

Soon after the elections Mexico made the headlines: unilateral moratorium was declared, triggering the debt crisis of the eighties in several other countries. The most important point here was that the entire financial situation of the country had not even been an issue during the presidential campaign of 1982. The opposition candidates had made attempts to attract the voters' attention on this matter, but the issue was little understood by the public (and probably by the candidates themselves); the media systematically concealed the nature and urgency of the problem. Miguel de la Madrid was elected with a huge majority of votes with the help of the power machinery of the ruling party, the PRI. Once again, the Mexican electorate rewarded the ruling party with a well-deserved victory.

During the de la Madrid administration, Mexico continued interest payments on its external debt: US$70 billion dollars were paid for this concept during his six years as president.[1] Social expenditures were cut drastically, triple digit inflation rates were attained (and brought down only in 1988), real wages dropped sharply, and the economy lapsed into a profound crisis.

At the beginning of his administration, Miguel de la Madrid diagnosed Mexico's ills as follows:

a) excessive indebtedness originated in insufficient domestic savings;
b) lack of competitiveness of the domestic economy;
c) structural disequilibria between agriculture, industry, and service sectors.

In order to solve these problems, a "modernizing strategy" designed to increase domestic savings and increase competitiveness of industries in order to avoid excessive dependency on foreign financial resources was deployed. The strategy was to unfold in three directions:

a) privatization,
b) opening the economy and deregulation, and
c) industrial conversion.

Miguel de la Madrid inherited a house in flames; the debt problem (with the high interest rates of the eighties) haunted his entire administration, as well as new reductions of oil prices (for example in 1985-86). So, perhaps it would be asking too much to expect positive results from his six years in power.

The situation with the Salinas administration is different for at least two important reasons. First, the main lines of the strategy were already in place: Mexico already had become a member of the General Agreement on Tariffs and Trade (GATT), deregulation and privatization had already started. Second, the international economic environment was more benign, with lower interest rates in the international financial markets so the debt burden was less demanding. It is important to keep these differences in mind when evaluating the performance of the Salinas administration.

---

[1]   Incidentally, this high external debt burden was partly the result of high interest rates predominating in the world's financial markets. The upward trend in interest rates was, in turn, greatly influenced by the pressure exerted in international financial markets by the United States Government in order to finance its fiscal deficit (while strict control was kept over the relevant monetary variables). As is well known, part of the fiscal deficit was due to military expenditures, although this was not the most important factor explaining the rise of the fiscal deficit of the U.S.

3. THE SALINAS ADMINISTRATION: 1988-1994

There are several myths about the Salinas administration. One is related to its role in "modernizing" the economy, the other to its relation with old hardliners of the PRI. The plot of the story is simple: in modernizing the economy, Salinas inflicted heavy costs on the old party bosses who rapidly became his enemies. In fact, the economy was deregulated and opened to international trade and investments, but this only brought along a mediocre performance in terms of growth. Increased inequality within Mexico and high vulnerability *vis-à-vis* the rest of the world were two of the dire consequences of these so-called structural reforms. In addition, insofar as the PRI is concerned, the old power structure was not changed and the old party bosses are still around.

The economic successes of the Salinas administration normally mentioned in the media were the following:

a) control of inflation: from 159 percent in 1987 to 8 percent in 1993.
b) balanced budget: surplus of 0.5 percent of Gross Domestic Product (GDP) in 1992.
c) privatization: more than 200 public enterprises privatized.
d) NAFTA successfully negotiated and ratified.
e) deregulation of the economy.

The next sections evaluate these apparent successes together with other aspects of the Salinas administration.

3.1   INFLATION

Harnessing inflation was undoubtedly the most important positive aspect of the Salinas administration, although the trend to reduce inflation started at the end of the de la Madrid administration. As the 1988 elections approached, the Government of Mexico (GOM) implemented a "social pact" with private enterprise, labor unions, and peasant organizations designed to control inflation and stabilize the economy. One key element in the pact was the contraction of public spending which generated a primary fiscal surplus (current revenues minus current expenditures excluding interest on debt) for that year. The "Pacto" became the key instrument during the Salinas regime to keep inflation under control. In addition, wage lags were introduced, contracting domestic demand. Public sector rates and prices for services were increased, subsidies reduced drastically, and the exchange rate was kept stable. As a result of this shock therapy, inflation decreased by mid-1988 to a 30 percent annualized rate (2.5 percent monthly). From here, the Salinas administration maintained a series of renewed "social pacts" with analogous objectives bringing inflation down to 7 percent in 1993 (unofficial estimates are slightly higher).

Inflation is the equivalent of a regressive tax system that negatively affects real wages in the low-income brackets of the income pyramid. Thus, a successful anti-inflation campaign has much going for it. The need to curb inflation was also seen as the way to fix the rate of exchange of the Mexican peso, something which would have multiple effects in the economy (further contributing to reduce inflationary expectations and consolidating the openness of the economy).

In fact, inflation was controlled in a very dogmatic way. The main elements in the task of reducing inflation were a drastic reduction in public expenditures, and a severe contraction of aggregate demand via a contraction of wages and credit. The contraction of wages took place as a deliberate policy objective.[2] The social cost of this policy cannot be underestimated. Even the private sector's own assessment acknowledges that the key factor behind this result is "the control over the main relative prices, particularly labor" and that this has had a high cost for investment, growth, and employment.

During the de la Madrid administration a trade surplus was the net result of this contraction of economic activity, and the peso was undervalued for much of the period 1982-1988. The Salinas administration kept the first two elements of the anti-inflationary policy, but as deregulation of trade policies intensified, the trade surplus disappeared. The trade deficit has been financed by foreign savings and this is the real foundation of the anti-inflationary success. But the inflow of foreign savings is essentially due to the high interest rates that reward preference for Mexico; these same high interest rates have had an extremely negative effect on economic activity. Even today the average real rate of interest in Mexico is 25 percent.

In more than one way, abatement of inflation rates does not rest on solid domestic foundations: if external vulnerability is not reduced, successes in the inflation front may evaporate rapidly. A devaluation would be needed if pressure from the external sector could not be reduced. And the expectations of a devaluation make the prospect of capital flight a real threat. International reserves of Mexico were hailed as another success of the Salinas regime, but by 1993 it was clear they would not stand a speculative attack on the peso. The crisis in December was sufficient proof of the extreme vulnerability of the reduction in the rate of inflation.

---

[2]   See testimony by the Minister of Finance in Aspe, *El camino mexicano hacia la transformación económica* (México: Fondo de Cultura Económica, 1993).

3.2 BALANCED BUDGET

A balanced budget was another cornerstone of the Salinas administration. It was seen essentially as an instrument in the struggle to curb inflation through the series of "pactos" that were promoted by the GOM. The main policy instruments used to reach a balanced budget (in fact, with a primary surplus of 0.5 percent of GDP in 1993) were the following:

i)   reduction of public spending,
ii) privatization of public enterprises,
iii) increase of fiscal revenues, and
iv) stabilization of the rate of exchange.

The reduction of interest rates in the international market, as well as the modest results of the Brady Plan, also contributed positively in this respect.

In assessing this result, it must be understood that the reduction of public spending is not necessarily a good measure and should, under most circumstances, be considered a temporary instrument (especially when the economy is undergoing a radical readjustment process as a result of the abrupt termination of protectionist policies). The most important element behind the zero deficit budget is the reduction of public spending in strategic areas of the economy. If Mexico were to become a viable open economy, the adjustment process would require a long-term commitment to establish the required base to accomplish the successful transition. The issue of public expenditures is not only one of quantities, but of qualitatively good policies where inter-industrial linkages are consolidated, agricultural production is strengthened, and the role of the service sector is streamlined. All of this has to be carried out together with increments in productivity which is conditioned by the incorporation of new technologies in the economy. The capacity to assimilate new technologies and to acquire technological capabilities can be insured only with a highly trained and capable work force. Public spending in education in Mexico is lagging far beyond the needs that a competitive open economy would demand. Finally, expenditures in research and development have not been able to recover the levels of the early 1980s and they barely reach a mere 0.4 percent of GDP.

Fiscal revenues were increased, and this is an important achievement in an economy with generalized tax evasion. But part of the increment is due to increased tariffs and rates charged for public services. Another part is due to the value-added tax which is regressive in nature.

Stabilizing the rate of exchange reduced interest payments (as a percentage of nominal GDP) on the public external debt and further contributed to reduce inflation. However, eventually this quasi-fixed parity resulted in the over-valuation of the Mexican peso. The disaster in December 1994 is intimately related to this point.

3.3 THE EXTERNAL CONSTRAINT: CURRENT ACCOUNT DEFICIT AND EXTERNAL DEBT

In the early years of the Salinas regime it was said that its major success would always be the renegotiation of the external debt in 1989. This was achieved through the auspices of the Brady Plan (and thanks to the primary fiscal surplus): under the renegotiation, savings of up to US$1.5 billion per year in interest payments were attained, together with a reduction of some US$7 billion in outstanding capital, and, finally, the conversion of a significant part of the debt (about US$35 billion) with banks in several industrial countries into thirty-year bonds secured by a purchase of U.S. treasury bonds.

At the end of the Salinas regime few GOM officials dared talk about the evolution of the external debt. Interest payments on the debt (which peaked at US$13 billion in 1982) settled at US$7 or $8 billion on average during the Salinas years. This represented a share of the foreign exchange earnings which is considered manageable (approximately 15 percent), but in view of the requirements to balance the current account deficit, it still may contribute negatively to the vulnerability of Mexico's external accounts. In addition, should interest payments rise once again, the burden will play a more important role (although it is hoped that new loans were negotiated under better terms than in the past, they still are linked to floating rates of interest). Finally, the implications of growing indebtedness of the private sector have not been clearly understood. We return below to the debt question in the new economic context after the December 1994 crisis.

As a proportion of GDP domestic savings dropped from 12.8 percent in 1981 to 5.3 percent in 1993. External sources of finance now represent 56 percent of total savings in 1993 (against 31 percent in 1981). This suggests that dependency on foreign savings is worse today than it was in 1982. As one can see, an enormous amount of foreign savings are required to attain a modest rate of growth for the economy. Is it possible to maintain this inflow of financial resources?

The difference in profitability between the Mexican stock market and other markets has eroded gradually: in 1993 the price/profitability ratio between issues in the Mexican Bolsa as 17.8 percent, and in the New York Stock Exchange, 21.5 percent. As a result, the Salinas administration resorted to high interest rates on its public debt in order to attract foreign capital: in so doing it has damaged the financial health of innumerable small and medium-sized Mexican firms. It is not surprising that Goldman Sachs and Standard & Poors recently have stated that Mexico will not get its investment degree until pressure from its external constraints is reduced.

3.4   PRIVATIZATION, NAFTA, AND DEREGULATION

These three items should be seen as instruments in a economic strategy, not as goals. The case of NAFTA is particularly important: it became urgently required during the last years of the Salinas regime due to the compelling need for foreign savings in order to cover the current account deficit. The U.S. administration sensed this and was able to extract as many concessions from the Mexican side as was possible.

Privatization was carried out under rather shady schemes in several important instances (telephone company, banks). The privatization of banks generated the creation of twenty financial groups made up of insurance companies and stock dealers, which have increased at their leisure the cost of financial intermediation. In any event, that recourse is now gone and it will not be possible to rely on this in the future to balance the budget.

The massive drive towards privatization involved more than US$20.5 billion dollars in government assets between 1990-1992. This provided the government with a flow of cash with which to meet all sorts of obligations. This allowed for a moderate downward trend in rates of interest and, together with the expansion of the money base, fostered the growth of the economy. In addition, foreign capital flows were enhanced as a result of increased deregulation and the reduction of the size of the public sector.

Contrary to the arguments used to support these measures, the Mexican economy failed to grow at an adequate pace and in a sustainable manner as a result of these policies. It is important to point out that the predictions of the computable general equilibrium (CGE) models used during the NAFTA debate in the United States failed to materialize. These models, built on a theoretical construct that implies free trade is mutually beneficial, predict welfare gains from trade liberalization as a normal outcome.

But the same goes for the forecasts based on CGE models regarding export potential, employment, and income distribution. It should be remembered that Walrasian CGE models are based on two fundamental assumptions which are unjustified: the absence of a distinct macroeconomic problem and the efficiency of flexible prices in clearing all markets. The use and abuse of these models may have led to totally misleading conclusions during the NAFTA debate, but the bad news is that GOM advisers have an irreducible faith in the results of the various runs of the models. Some isolated references on these models are made below.

3.5   INCOME DISTRIBUTION AND EMPLOYMENT

Out of a labor force of approximately 34 million people, the *official* figure for open unemployment is 3 percent (but see below). The CIEMEX-Wharton predictions estimate 10 percent of the total labor force, or 3.5 million persons. In fact, open unemployment may rise as high as 12-15 percent partly due to demographic inertia (reflecting the 3 percent rate of growth of population sixteen years ago). Approximately one million persons enter the labor market every year.

During the decade 1982-1992 formal employment has not expanded significantly. There were 21 million people employed in 1983, and 22.6 in 1992 (this figure probably fell somewhat in 1993 as the recession intensified). In view of this, it is possible to fully appreciate one of the monumental deficiencies in most of the CGE models used to assess and even predict the impact of NAFTA. Because the models are based on the premise that the economy is in its full-employment position, one of the most important and serious economic problems is simply assumed away.

In its struggle to counter inflation the GOM disposed of a formidable instrument denied to other governments in Latin America: the corporatist organization of the state party, the PRI. Through this system of political control, ceilings were negotiated (imposed) which put the evolution of contractual wages below inflation. In addition, the sluggish growth rates of the economy translated into a mediocre performance in job generation. It is not surprising, then, to observe that participation of wages in GDP went down from 37 percent in 1982 to 25.5 percent in 1993, according to data provided by the *Instituto Nacional de Estadística*, Geografía e Informática INEGI, Sistema de Cuentas Nacionales.

Minimum wages have contracted without interruption during the two administrations and they now have 47 percent of the purchasing power they had in 1982; contractual wages lost 40 percent of their purchasing power. This has led to impressive transformations in the composition of employment, with a dramatic growth of unstable, part-time employment. It is no surprise to observe that the average number of workers per family increased from 1.4 to 1.5 between 1977 and 1984, and to 1.6 in 1992. This seems to support the claim that a minimum wage is not enough to support one family.[3]

---

[3]   A recent study on social exclusion in Mexico shows that in 1988, 4.78 minimum wages were required to purchase one standard basket to satisfy basic needs. Assuming the official statistics on inflation rates, in 1992 only the highest wages in the manufacturing sector were able to cover 90 percent of the basket's value. Salas, "Income, Employment and Gender: Three Dimensions of Exclusion in Mexico," *Working Papers Series*, (DI-IV-93) (Science

Officials close to the Salinas administration claim that real wages started to recover during the last four years. Average salaries of employees in the manufacturing sector do show a slight recovery. But it is difficult to accept that wages recovered. Official calculations leading to this conclusion are based on the concept of "average compensation per employed person" for the firms covered in the monthly Industrial Surveys (which cover a non-representative sample of 3,000 establishments responsible for more than 65 percent value added of manufacturing). Thus, part of the recovery in wages is explained by undue inclusion of salaries and fringe benefits accruing to employees of the larger establishments in the manufacturing sector in the calculations. Also brought into the calculation of real income accruing to workers are severance payments, funeral costs paid by firms, etc.

Official statistics report 3 percent of open unemployment. In 1994, however, open unemployment increased to 6 percent of the labor force, and employment in the manufacturing industries decreased by 4-5 percent (going from approximately 1 million workers to 950,000) according to the Monthly Manufacturing Survey, INEGI. In addition, there are several problems with this figure. It refers only to urban unemployment (in approximately thirty cities covered by the INEGI surveys). Open unemployment is defined as that part of the economically active population (EAP) currently unemployed and actively searching for a job. This is involuntary unemployment *stricto sensu*. If you worked one hour during the previous reference period (one week) then you are not unemployed. Finally, these statistics conceal the extraordinary rise of unstable and precarious employment in activities of very low productivity. Underemployment is currently estimated to be as high as 35 percent of EAP. Underemployment has risen dramatically in Mexico.

In total, underemployment and open unemployment can be estimated to be as high as 40-45 percent of EAP. This is an intolerable burden and cannot be sustained. This very high estimate seems to be corroborated by other data. Calculations based on official statistics indicate that 54 percent of families have monthly incomes below one minimum wage (about US$135). The size of the domestic market is now dangerously reduced and composed of the 21 percent of families whose mean monthly income is above three minimum wages (US$405).

Income distribution has become more skewed in the last twelve years. Functional income distribution evolved during the last decade as follows:

and Technology Program, El Colegio de México, 1993).

Figure 1

	1981	*1991*
Profits (operational surplus)	52.8%	61.6%
Labor remunerations	42.6%	29.0%

SOURCE: *Instituto Nacional de Estadística, Geografía e Informática (INEGI).*

The degree of income concentration also becomes apparent in the following data on family income distribution (all data from INEGI, 1984, 1992): 40 percent of households with lower incomes saw their share reduced from 14.3 percent in 1984 to 12.6 percent in 1992; middle income brackets also suffered a reduction in their share. The top ten percent saw its share increase from 32 percent to 38 percent between 1984 and 1992. Using figures for the 1989-1992 period does not change the picture, although the rates of change tend to slow down as the effects of rigidities become stronger (ceilings and floors are reached).

The Gini coefficient (measuring the surface of the between the Lorenz curve and the equidistribution line) increased as follows:

Table I. INCOME DISTRIBUTION IN MEXICO

	(Gini coefficients)		
Year	*Total income*	*Monetary*	*Non-monetary*
1984	0.4292	0.4652	0.5506
1989	0.4694	0.4889	0.5921
1992	0.4749	0.5086	0.5404

SOURCE: J. Boltvinik, Gasto Social, distribución del ingreso y desigualdad en México, in P. Moncayo & J. Woldenberg (eds.), Las perspectivas del desarollo Sustenable en México (1994).

Income distribution has never been very good in Mexico. The last twelve years have made it worse. But Mr. Salinas claimed that under his administration, the trend towards greater Gini coefficients had been checked. The truth of the matter is different: only the Gini coefficient for the non-monetary component of income became smaller between 1989-1992. But what is the non-monetary component of income? The official definition includes under this item such things as imputation of a monthly rental when individuals own their own house, and gifts in specie received by the family. This is quite misleading of the evolution of income, opening the door for arbitrary manipulation of data.

This is an important aspect of economic reality which was radically distorted in the computable general equilibrium (CGE) models used in the days of the NAFTA debate. These models assume that marginal productivity, which is determined via the market-clearing input decisions of profit-maximizing firms which act as price-takers, is the sole element determining shares of income re-warding factors. The restrictive nature of these assumptions disqualifies CGE models as tools for policy. In the case of the Mexican setting, CGE models ignore the capacity of the Mexican government to implement a restrictive incomes policy with severe wage constraints. Finally, most of the CGE models that were used in the NAFTA debate assume that each economy consists of a single homogeneous type of consumer. This allows the model to ignore the effects of changes in income distribution patterns on aggregate welfare and out-put. In the case of Mexico, one of the distortions brought about by income con-centration already may be having an impact on the structure of imports and do-mestic output of light manufacturing industries.

3.6   SOCIAL EXPENDITURES AND POVERTY

The anti-poverty program *Solidaridad* was highly publicized as a successful and innovative scheme of the Salinas government. This program was a mixture of self-help schemes and traditional social expenditures. The net result was praised by many, especially insofar as self-help was presented as a process leading to greater self-respect and a deeper sense of personal dignity. There are, of course, some positive results. Corruption plagued the program, and the use of resources in a highly discriminatory manner transformed social spending into a more effi-cient instrument of the PRI. In many cases, rights were transformed into some-thing resembling privileges or rewards for political allegiance. To present the program as a new approach leading to increased self-respect and dignity is a bit exaggerated in a country where mean schooling age is only five years (and a very poor educational service). In any event, an evaluation of the program must take into account the following points:

First, the budgetary items covered by this program were in existence under previous administrations. In fact, as can be seen in Table II, the resources com-mitted to these budgetary items in 1980 were higher than those earmarked for *Solidaridad* in 1993:

Table II. EXPENDITURES IN *SOLIDARIDAD* AND REGIONAL DEVELOPMENT

Year	Millions of Constant 1980 U.S. Dollars
1980	1,172
1981	2,255
1988	283
1992	1,148
1993	1,302

SOURCE: SHCP, *Presupuesto de Egresos de la Federación y Gasto Programable* (several years).

Second, a piece of information seldom considered is the high proportion of the budget of *Solidaridad* going to publicity and maintaining a high profile (organizing campaigns and visits by GOM officials, etc.). Estimates are difficult, but it is clear that this was not a negligible component of *Solidaridad's* budget.

According to official data (INEGI), 44 percent of the population of Mexico currently lives below the poverty line. Total population of Mexico as of mid-1994 was 93 million: this means more than 40 million persons live below the poverty line. It is not surprising that during the last twelve years infant mortality as a result of malnutrition increased *220 percent* for children between one and four years old. For children below the age of one year, this indicator increased by more than *120 percent*. In 1980 there were 13 million children and young people between the ages of five and twenty-five years without any school attendance whatsoever. In 1990 this number rose to 15 million. An official publication sets this figure at 24.2 million![4]

4. BALANCE: WHERE IS THE MEXICAN ECONOMY HEADING?

The main objectives of the de la Madrid-Salinas administrations were not attained. Not only that, in many ways the Mexican economy is now more vulnerable than it was in 1982.

4.1 GROWTH: PAST AND FUTURE

As can be appreciated in Table III, the overall performance of the economy during the Salinas administration was quite disappointing.

---

[4] SEP-ANUIES, Datos Básicos de la Educacíon Superior, 1992-1992.

Table III. REAL GROWTH RATE OF GDP, MEXICO

Year	Rate of Growth (percent)
1987	1.5
1988	1.1
1989	2.9
1990	3.9
1991	3.6
1992	2.6
1993	0.4
1994(a)	2.0
1995(a)	-4.5
1994(b)	3.1
1995(b)	-2.0

Average annual growth rate (a) 1.5%
(b) 1.9%

SOURCE: 1989-1993, Banco de México, *Indicadores Económicos*. 1994(a), author's estimate based on INEGI, *Encuesta mensual industrial*; 1994(b), *Lineamientos de política económica, Poder Ejecutivo Federal*, December 9, 1994; 1995(a) author's estimate; 1995(b), official GOM estimate.

In 1993 the official inflation rate was 8 percent and every indicator for the stagnant Mexican economy performed poorly. The mediocre rates of growth conceal myriad other phenomena. Particularly important is the impact of the very high real interest rates which have predominated in the Mexican context during the last five years as an effort to keep capital inflow and prevent capital flight.

Gross Domestic Product (GDP) growth rate for 1994 was 3.1 percent according to the President's Report to the Mexican congress outlining economic policy guidelines for the 1995 fiscal budget. This figure is difficult to believe and may be more related to the last-ditch attempts of Mr. Salinas to bolster the record of his administration. Public expenditures in programs such as PROCAMPO increased during 1994 (a crucial election year), but they could not have produced this overall result. Open unemployment increased by a dramatic 80 percent during 1994, as revealed by the monthly industrial surveys of INEGI. Considering past data on unemployment and industrial output, it is possible to estimate a growth rate of approximately 2 percent in 1994.

The evolution of per capita GDP is revealing. In addition, per capita GDP depends on the population data used. The 1990 Population Census returns show 81.3 million persons as of mid-March. An adjustment of 500,000 persons has to be added for comparability (data from previous census were given for July). In addition, about 3.5 million persons should be added, according to estimates by demographers (at El Colegio de México) due to underreporting errors. With absolute population growth at about 2 million per year, mid-1994 population would

stand at 93 million.[5] If these unofficial but more reliable estimates for population growth are used, GDP per capita remained stagnant in 1992 and actually
dropped by 1.6 percent in 1993. This compares rather poorly with performance
during the protectionist era when GDP per capita rose at an annual average of 3
percent for more than two decades, between 1955-1975. Prospects for the rest of
the decade are not extremely bright. In the best possible scenario (assuming a
sustained and healthy takeoff of the U.S. economy) rates of growth of 3-4 percent per annum will be achieved. But even this prospect is not guaranteed due to
the constraints described below.

4.2   SERVICING THE EXTERNAL DEBT

The crisis which erupted on December 20 has brought back to life the phantom
of the external debt crisis. Liabilities with the rest of the world are summarized
in Table IV, comparing August 1982 with the situation in 1994 and early 1995.

Table IV. MEXICO'S EXTERNAL DEBT

	1982	*1993*	*1994*	*1-XII-95*
External Debt	78,000	118,000	135,300	171,036
Public	57,400	80,000	97,800(a)	124,000(b)
Private	20,500	38,000	37,500	48,000
Banks	n.a.	n.a.	n.a.	28,600
Firms	n.a.	n.a.	n.a.	18,436(c)

Rate of growth of GDP during 1987-1994:   16.1%
Rate of growth of total real liabilities: 70.0%

(a)   Includes portfolio investments in government bonds nominally denominated in pesos but redeemable at the going rate
      of exchange against the U.S. dollar (i.e., Tesobonos) for an equivalent US$20 billion.
(b)   Includes US$30 billion IMF and Exchange Stabilisation Fund of the U.S. Treasury for the financial rescue in 1995.
(c)   External liabilities of firms in the Mexico Stock Exchange (*Bolsa de Valores de México*).

SOURCE: "Informes Trimestrales sobre la situación de las finanzas públicas," Secretaría de Hacienda y Crédito Públi-
          co; "Indicadores Económicos," Banco de México. Data for 1995 (last column) from Carlos Marichal, "Polí-
          ticas alternativas para el manejo de la deuda externa mexicana en 1995-1996" (mimeograph) (El Colegio de
          México, Aug. 1995).

Servicing outstanding external debt is incompatible with the objective of
sustainable economic growth for the Mexican economy. In 1995 interest payments will be no less than US$13 billion; in fact, in spite of the favorable trade

---

[5]   These figures affect several other statistical calculations, most notably for unemployment, per capita social expenditures, etc. As the officials responsible for the 1990 census
were later responsible for the federal voters' registry, the under-reporting also may be
related to manipulation of the federal voters' register used in the 1994 election. This is
something that has to be analyzed carefully.

balance, an important current account deficit will result precisely because of the heavy burden posed by the external debt.

4.3   TOWARDS EXPORT-LED GROWTH?

Exports have expanded spectacularly, but so have imports. This has generated a huge trade deficit of more than US$21 billion in 1993. Among other factors, this is the result of the strong bias in favor of intermediate inputs (the only explanation behind the slow growth in the trade deficit between 1992 and 1993 was the stagnation of the Mexican economy).

Manufactured exports are concentrated in motor vehicles, engines and auto parts, machinery in general, chemical products, iron and steel, building materials, electronic appliances. Other important items are cement and glass. Exports by main groups show the importance of manufactures:

Table V. EXPORTS BY BRANCH OF ECONOMIC ACTIVITY. 1985-1994

Year	Oil	Farm Products	Mineral	Manufacturing	Total
1985	14.7	1.4	.5	4.9	21.6
1988	6.6	1.6	.6	11.5	20.5
1989	7.7	1.7	.6	12.6	22.8
1990	9.9	2.1	.6	13.9	26.8
1991	8.0	2.3	.5	15.7	26.8
1992	8.2	2.1	.3	16.7	27.5
1993	7.3	2.5	.2	19.8	21.8
1994	4.7	1.9	.1	15.6	22.3

NOTE: All figures in US$ billions.
SOURCE: Banco de México, *Indicadores Económicos* (INEGI).

The high rate of growth of manufactures in exports is related to the inflow of direct foreign investment. It has its counterpart in the imports of capital goods and intermediate goods carried out by these firms.

Table VI. STRUCTURE OF MEXICAN MANUFACTURING EXPORTS BY MAIN GROUPS, 1994

Item	Millions of U.S. Dollars	Percent
Total exports FOB	60,833.40	100.00
Maquiladoras	26,269.30	43.2
Non-maquiladoras	34,564.10	56.8
Agriculture	2,221.00	3.7
Livestock and fish	457.40	0.8
Extractive industries	6,942.50	11.4
Manufact. industries	51,078.30	84.0
Other products	134.20	0.2

SOURCE: *Estadísticas del Comercio Exterior de México*, Vol. XVII (12). INEGI, 1994.

Imports of manufacturing industries can be broken down as follows:

Table VII. IMPORTS BY TYPE OF PRODUCT, 1989-1994

Year	Capital Goods	Intermediate Inputs	Consumer Goods	Total
1989	8.4	24.0	5.6	38.0
1992	11.4	39.3	7.4	58.2
1993	10.9	43.1	7.5	61.5
1994	13.2	52.2	9.0	74.4

NOTE: All figures in billions of current U.S. dollars.
SOURCE: Banco de México, *Informe Anual*; *Estadísticas del Comercio Exterior Mexicano*, Vol. XVII (8), 1994, INEGI.

The structure of imports is quite revealing. The share of intermediate inputs has increased at a faster rate of growth (more than 20 percent in 1993-94). It is also due to some of the policy instruments used by the Ministry of Trade and Industrial Promotion (SECOFI). Especially important in this context is the program on temporary imports and exports (PITEX). Also responsible are the schedules of tariff reduction and phasing out contained in NAFTA: intermediate goods and capital goods were among the items with the most rapid phasing out of tariffs. This is contrary to the industrial policy followed by most successful newly industrialized countries, in particular South Korea; but it was a deliberate choice in Mexico's position *via-à-vis* the NAFTA negotiations.

This highly skewed structure of imports also is caused by the disruption and interruption of most forward and backward linkages in the industrial matrix. Abruptly opening the economy without any selectivity has caused the closing of a high number of firms which catered to the domestic market for intermediate goods; these firms, with their inefficiencies, were the result of the protectionist policies which existed in Mexico since the 1940s. Today, instead of transforming these firms into a streamlined nucleus of an industrial base, getting rid of the set of protectionist policies left them in a state of extreme vulnerability. This is especially true if we consider the high cost of credit these firms encountered during the period 1988-1994.

4.4 THE *"MAQUILADORA"* INDUSTRY

The *maquiladora* subsector already has contributed significantly to the performance of the export sector, but its net contribution should not be overestimated. According to recent SECOFI data the *maquiladora* subsector is already responsible for more than 55 percent of total exports, but its share of total imports is also quite spectacular (see Table VII). The employment generation potential of the *maquiladoras* may be important but not the pie in the sky official press releases describe: 180,000 new jobs were created in the last six years. This is good performance for one sector, but we may not count on this sector alone to solve the unemployment problem.

Table VIII. THE MAQUILADORA INDUSTRY

Year	Imports	Exports	Balance	Employment
1987	5,507	7,105	1,598	305,253
1988	7,808	10,146	2,338	369,489
1989	9,328	12,329	3,001	418,533
1990	10,321	13,873	3,552	447,606
1991	11,782	15,833	4,050	467,352
1992	13,936	18,680	4,743	505,698
1993	16,443	21,853	5,410	540,927
1994	20,493	26,269	5,775	563,954

NOTE: Figures in millions of dollars.
SOURCE: *Estadística de la industria maquiladora de exportación*, 1989-1993. INEGI, 1994.

The *maquiladora* plants operating in Mexico have been extolled as an important contribution to the generation of employment. During the six years of the Salinas administration, *maquiladora* plants created 194,000 direct jobs. Once again, because the linkages with the rest of the economy are weak, indirect jobs are negligible. But, in addition, these jobs have several features which reveal the *maquiladora* program does not offer a very attractive response to Mexico's employment problem. For the most part, employment in the *maquiladora* plants is not very stable; its temporary nature of employment in the *maquiladoras* has been well documented.[6] Besides, the level of average wages and labor compensation in the *maquiladora* plants is lower than in the rest of the manufacturing sector. Thus, the *maquiladora* program will not provide an answer to the employment program and, in fact, it is possible that the program's benefits may be surpassed by the social costs involved in terms of the quality of life in the communities with strong presence of *maquiladoras*.

On top of this, there is the heated debate around the methodological change introduced in 1991 dealing with the use of gross flows of merchandise, instead of the traditional and more logical method which took into account only the net value (added) of exports. With the change in methodology, SECOFI was able to claim in the press a dramatic increment in "exports" by the *maquiladoras*. It must be recalled that imported inputs used by the *maquiladora* industry in its totality represent 98.2 percent of total inputs.

The behavior of the *maquiladora* model is not surprising: while *maquiladora*

[6] Red Mexicana de Acción Frente al Libre Comercio (RMALC), *Tratado de Libre Comercio de América del Norte* (Análisis, Crítica y Propuesta) (1993).

exports expand at rather impressive rates, the impact on the rest of the economy is marginal or practically negligible. This is what one would expect from an industry which has very limited linkages with the economy. If local inputs are 2 percent of the final value of goods exported by the *maquiladoras*, the multiplier effect derived from this productive activity is not to be found within the Mexican economy. This explains why, although the *maquiladora* industry may find important competitive advantages in Mexico, especially in terms of very depressed real wages (and eventually, in terms of lax enforcement of local environmental legislation), it cannot provide the needed dynamic impulses for the rest of the economy. This is why there may be years with rapid growth of non-traditional exports, with very little impact on the growth rate of the entire economy.

Table IX. THE MAQUILADORA MODEL: RATES OF GROWTH OF GDP AND EXPORTS

Year	GDP	Total	Non-maquiladora Exports(a)	Maquiladora Exports
1987	1.5	26.5	26.8	25.8
1988	1.1	11.2	0.2	42.8
1989	2.9	14.5	11.1	21.5
1990	3.9	15.7	17.4	12.5
1991	3.6	4.8	0.06	14.1
1992	2.6	8.2	2.4	17.9
1993	0.4	12.3	9.1	16.9
Averages	2.2	13.3	9.5	21.6

(a) Non-maquiladora exports include oil exports.

NOTE: All figures in percentages.
SOURCE: Author's calculations based on data from Banco de México.

But the *maquiladora* model does not stop with the in-bond plants located in Mexico. More than 70 percent of total imports are intermediate goods. This figure shows that, because of the disruption in the forward and backward linkages, and because of the use of policy instruments to promote temporary imports, the *maquiladora* syndrome is extending to the entire economy. In fact, as we shall see below, this type of arrangement already is dominating the single most important exporting industry of the Mexican economy, the automotive complex.

It is not possible to accurately calculate the trade balance of each branch of the manufacturing sector. Foreign trade statistics are presented in such a way that branch exports can be obtained, net of *maquiladoras*, at the two-digit level. If one needs analogous information at the three-or four-digit level, this exercise is not possible. But even more disturbing is the impossibility of identifying imports carried by or attributable to a specific branch of industry. Thus, intra-industry trade may be captured by examining foreign trade statistics, but because data on inter-industry trade is organized along different principles, calculating the net trade balance of specific branches is not possible.

Data on imports exists in such a form that the trade balance of the automobile industry can be estimated. In the case of the automobile industry, data on imports by industry origin allows us to identify a few of the most important sources of imports. According to Table IX the trade balance of the industry for 1993 and 1994 represents a small deficit of -391 and -633 respectively. These figures are a good indicator of the weight of imports by this branch which has been touted as one of (if not the) most important exporter in Mexico's manufactures. The items deserve some discussion.

Table X. STRUCTURE OF EXPORTS OF MANUFACTURING INDUSTRIES IN MEXICO, 1994

Item	Total Exports	Exports Without Maquiladora(a)	Percent
Total manufacturing industries	51,078	24,809	100.0%
Food, drinks, tobacco	1,896	1,652	6.7%
Textiles, apparel, leather	3,256	1,150	4.6%
Wood industries	586	267	1.1%
Paper, print, and publications	562	229	0.9%
Oil products	545	545	2.2%
Petrochemicals	263	263	1.1%
Chemicals	2,756	2,482	10.0%
Plastic products, rubber	1,046	294	1.2%
Non-metallic minerals	1,215	854	3.4%
Iron and steel	1,535	1,224	4.9%
Metallurgical industries	1,085	1,010	4.1%
Metal products, machinery and equipment	35,327	14,677	59.2%
Other industries	989	167	0.7%

(a)   Figures in this column are the result of subtracting maquiladora exports from total exports of manufacturing *cum* maquiladora exports as reported in Table XI.

NOTE: Export figures in millions of U.S. dollars.
SOURCE: Foreign Trade Statistics of Mexico, Vol. XVII (12), 1994, INEGI, tables 15 and 22.

In the first place, the vast majority of the exports by firms in this industrial complex (final production and assembly plants, medium and small auto-parts manufacturers) are captured here. It is possible that some exports carried out by the automobile complex are not included, but this must be a marginal amount. Secondly, imports by the automobile industrial complex are strongly underestimated here: the presentation of data allows us to identify and take into account imports which we know are carried out by the automobile manufacturers. But there are imports which we cannot identify and attribute to firms in this industrial complex: machine tools, jigs, dies, metalworking equipment, electrical machinery and equipment, loading and unloading equipment, etc. These imports appear under item "Machinery and equipment for sundry industries;" although it is not possible to provide a reliable estimate of this amount, it is clear that taking them into account would increase the negative contribution of the branch to the trade balance.

Table XI. AUTOMOTIVE INDUSTRIES: TRADE BALANCE, 1993-1994

	1993	*1994*
	Exports	
Automobile Industries	4,251	5,077
Trucks	670	830
Chassis w/ motors(b)	134	213
Motors for autos	1,302	1,778
Suspension bars	106	126
Auto parts	1,889	2,107
Total Exports	8,353	10,130
	Main Imports	
	1993	*1994*
Automobiles(a)	491	1,399
Trucks	33	34
Automobile chassis	9	50
Assembly material	6,439	6,733
Motors & auto parts	394	565
Spare parts autos & trucks	1,377	1,981
Transmissions	40	41
Total Main Exports	8,784	10,804
Balance, Exports-Imports for Automobile Industry	(431)	(674)

(a) Includes automobiles with special features.
(b) Chassis with motors for all types of vehicles.

SOURCE: Prepared by the author using *Estadísticas del comercio exterior de México*, Información preliminar, enero-agosto Vol. XVII, (12), 1994, INEGI.

Mexico's automobile industrial complex was the target of an explicit policy to strengthen backward linkages since the early 1960s. The story of these policies is not the object of this paper, but it should be noted that most of the auto-part industrial complex existing today is the result of those efforts to increase what has been known in Mexico as the "degree of national integration." Some of these policies remain legally in effect, but they have been brushed aside by the SECOFI in order to pursue negotiations for NAFTA. In fact, NAFTA includes a restriction on these types of measures (export performance and national integration are strongly restricted). The end result is that one single industry, the automobile industrial complex, is responsible for importing US$10,804 million in intermediate goods, representing more than 20 percent of total imports of intermediate goods carried out in 1994.

Of course, when analyzing data on exports by the automobile industrial complex, it is important to bear in mind that exports of automobiles, trucks, and motors are carried out by the big multinationals in this branch, while exports of auto parts are carried out by a group of firms which belong to a different category, both in terms of size as well as in their networks of marketing channels and financial versatility. A more detailed study should be able to show that the auto parts industries show a higher degree of national integration in total value added. But data for the big final producers (and assemblers) of cars and trucks will show the *maquiladora* syndrome has taken deep roots in this industry.

Another crucial aspect of manufactured goods exports is the very high degree of concentration in a few branches of industry. Only four groups are responsible for 84 percent of total exports of manufacturing industries: food, textiles and apparel, chemicals, and metal products. These groups can be reduced to a very small number of individual industries:

Figure 2

Food, drinks, tobacco	1,896
Textiles	3,256
Chemicals	2,756
Transport and communications	10,869
Electric and electronic	17,277
Subtotal	36,054

This subtotal represents 70 percent of total exports from all manufacturing industries. This is another reason for the little response the economy is having *vis-à-vis* export performance. In spite of the fact that exports grow, the economy remains unresponsive due to the lack of backward linkages of the exporting sectors with the rest of the economy. The detailed breakdown of export figures for all manufacturing industries is provided in Table XII.

Table XII. MANUFACTURING INDUSTRIES EXPORTS, 1994

Item	Millions of U.S. Dollars	Percent
Total manufacturing industries	51,078	100
Food, drinks, tobacco	1,896	3.7
Frozen shrimp	334	0.7
Beer	233	0.5
Fruit and vegetables	291	0.6
Tequila	157	0.3
Other	882	1.7
Textiles, apparel, leather	3,256	6.4
Leather goods	151	0.3
Cotton products	889	1.7
Silk and artificial fibers and products	689	1.3
Shoes	196	0.4
Synthetic fibers	537	1.1
Other	794	1.6
Wood industries	586	1.1
Veneer	183	0.4
Furniture	375	0.7
Other	28	0.05
Paper, print and publications	562	1.1
Books	120	0.2
Other	441	0.9

Oil products	544	1.1
Gas	113	0.2
Gas oil	128	0.3
Other	304	0.6
Petrochemicals	263	0.5
Ammonia	52	0.1
PVC	108	0.2
Ethylene	43	0.08
Polyethelene	19	0.04
Other	41	0.08
Chemicals	2,756	5.4
Hydrofluoric acid	62	0.1
Polycarboxilic acid	290	0.6
Colors and varnishes	161	0.3
Plastics and synthetic resins	440	0.9
Other	1,803	3.5
Plastic products, rubber	1,064	2.1
Tires	55	0.1
Synthetic resin and plastic goods	828	1.6
Other	182	0.4
Non-metallic minerals	1,215	2.4
Clay and porcelain goods	85	0.2
Cement	57	0.1
Bricks and tiles	105	0.2
Glass and glass products	668	1.3
Other	300	0.6
Iron and steel	1,535	3.0
Iron ingots and rods	582	1.1
Manufactured iron and steel	272	0.5
Tubes and pipes	301	0.6
Other	380	0.7
Metallurgical industries	1,085	2.1
Copper	296	0.6
Silver	214	0.4
Other	575	1.1
Metal products, machinery, and equipment	35,327	69.2
Agriculture	105	0.2
Railroads	20	0.0
Transport and communications	10,869	21.3
Automobiles, passenger	5,077	9.9
Automobiles, cargo	830	1.6
Motors for autos	1,778	3.5
Parts for autos	2,107	4.1
Other	1,078	2.1
Sundry industries	6,007	11.8
Bearings	152	0.3
Air conditioning equipment	251	0.5
Ovens and stoves	240	0.5
Faucets and valves	388	0.8
Typewriters	192	0.4
Data processing equipment	1,243	2.4
Parts for machinery	1,087	2.1
Other	2,453	4.8
Scientific equipment	652	1.3
Medical equipment	358	0.7
Other	294	0.6

Electric and electronic	17,277	33.8
Cables	2,930	5.7
Magnetic tapes and records	498	1.0
Electric motors	572	1.1
Electrical instruments	2,098	4.1
Radio and TV Parts	1,065	2.1
Parts, electric equipment	1,846	3.6
Refrigerators	205	0.4
Transformers	666	1.3
Other	7,397	14.5
Photo and optical	397	0.8
Photo and film equipment	248	0.5
Other	148	0.3
Other industries	989	1.9
Balloons	212	0.4
Toys and sporting goods	230	0.5
Other	547	1.1
Other goods not elsewhere included	134	0.3

SOURCE: *Estadísticas del Comercio Exterior de México*, Información Preliminar. Vol. XVII (12), 1994, INEGI.

There are several elements that must be considered carefully when assessing the importance of manufactured exports. First, their importance may be over-rated. In 1992 trade statistics were modified by the Banco de México in order to add the gross value of all *maquiladora* imports and exports to the trade balance (i.e., to conventional imports and exports). The trade ministry, SECOFI, was able to publicize extraordinary growth rates of exports and insist that the Mexican economy had become overnight an export-led growth machine, arguing that exports of manufactures now represented more than 60 percent of aggregate commodity exports, with oil exports making up only 30 percent.

A more cautious approach is warranted here. In fact, the net contribution of the *maquiladora* industry to Mexico's trade position has to be assessed with more precise data (see Table XIII).

Second, the concentration of exports in a few firms is rather intense and unhealthy. The largest 500 firms are responsible for 75 percent of total manufacturing exports according to *Informe Especial de Expansión*, 1994. Concentration among the firms in this group is even more intense. Most of the important ones are subsidiaries of multinational corporations in the high export branches (automobiles, engines, chemicals, electronics). It is possible that as much as 43 percent of total exports by manufacturing firms is due to subsidiaries of transnational corporations. This pattern is already leading to a two-tiered manufacturing sector where wholly-owned subsidiaries and joint ventures are able to perform adequately in the international markets, while medium and small domestic firms face serious difficulties as far as credit and technology are concerned. These medium-sized and small firms in the textile, footwear, leather, toys, furniture,

and food processing industries form a second tier of units; they have low productivity, low-quality goods, and are in jeopardy; the number of firms going into
bankruptcy every day is alarming. The failure to build more intense backward
linkages with the local manufacturing sector will seriously hamper the export
industries' ability to generate growth impulses for the entire manufacturing sector.

**Table XIII. ESTIMATES OF NET CONTRIBUTIONS OF THE MAQUILADORA
INDUSTRY TO MEXICO'S FOREIGN TRADE POSITION, 1994**

Item	Exports	Imports	Balance
Total maquiladoras in manufacturing industries	26,269.31	19,609.08	6,660.23
Food, drinks, tobacco	243.11	36.26	206.85
Textiles, apparel, leather	2,105.50	1,817.48	288.02
Wood industries	319.36	172.31	147.05
Paper print and publications	332.22	748.16	(415.94)
Oil products	-	11.62	(11.62)
Petrochemicals	-	14.06	(14.06)
Chemicals	274.27	562.17	(287.90)
Plastic products, rubber	770.63	2,009.27	(1,238.64)
Non-metallic minerals	361.21	285.90	75.31
Iron and Steel	310.75	1,277.43	(966.68)
Metallurgical industries	75.53	351.29	(275.76)
Metal products, machinery and equipment	20,650.83	12,073.45	8,577.38
Other industries	822.13	249.63	572.50

SOURCES: (a) *Sexto Informe de Gobierno*, Anexo (Banco de México); Foreign Trade Statistics of Mexico, Preliminary Information, Vol. XVII (12), 1994. INEGI.

Third, recent export performance has been concentrated in capital intensive
branches. The promise of more exports will materialize only through intensive
use of new flexible manufacturing technology. It was once thought that flexible
manufacturing could open new possibilities for exports from LDCs due to the
small size of production batches. It is clear now that small batches at the product
level do not necessarily entail the disappearance of scale economies at the plant
level. In addition, the requirements of competitive flexible manufacturing (in
terms of software, electronic equipment, communications for simultaneous decision-making in product design, production and marketing, etc.) make it more
capital intensive than most traditional technologies. The employment generation
potential of flexible manufacturing is not as significant as believed only a few
years ago.

Officials in the GOM have systematically confused the objectives of trade
policy with those of macroeconomic policies and industrial policy. For example,
imports are credited with bringing down inflation, but this is a silly way of putting things: the vulnerability of the external sector would, in the end, destroy the
base of any anti-inflation success. Industrial policy is defined by GOM officials
in SECOFI as deregulation of trade policies. If one looks at science and technology policies, for example, the GOM points at the new industrial property law

which is stronger than its U.S. counterpart in several respects (in compulsory licensing, for example). But Mexico does not even have the infrastructure to administer this patent law and the substantive patent examination process is carried out in the U.S. patent office.

There is a lot of evidence everywhere of countries engaging in interventionist policies (rather than relying on the free market) in order to capture some of the gains from economies of scale. That the interventionist approach has advantages is shown in recent trade theory,[7] in a large body of literature on business history,[8] and in general economic history[9] and policy.[10] Examples include the United States, which followed a protectionist road for much of the nineteenth century.

5. CONCLUDING REMARKS

The change in administration at the end of 1994 was marked by the December devaluation of the peso. An immediate result was a period of extraordinary instability in the foreign exchange and stock markets. As interest rates increased at a very rapid rate, firms were caught with dollar denominated debts and internal obligations they were unable to serve. The reaction of the new administration was swift, but unimaginative. A strict contractionist program was imposed, cutting public expenditures, pursuing a tight monetary policy, and contracting the real supply of domestic credit. Wages have been frozen in order to use nominal wages as an anchor in the new struggle against inflation.

In order to meet short-term financial obligations, the new administration entered into an agreement with the U.S. Department of the Treasury and the International Monetary Fund (IMF). The stabilization program includes US$20 billion from the Exchange Stabilization Fund, plus US$17.5 billion from the IMF. The agreement covers three forms of support for Mexico's embattled financial system: short-term swaps (90 days), medium-term swaps (5 years), and guarantees through which Mexico's obligations are covered for up to 10 years. Mexico is to use the support to retire, refinance, or restructure short-term obligations.

A strong package of conditions is linked to this assistance. Some of the new

---

[7] P. Krugman (ed.), *Strategic Trade Policy and the New International Economics* (1991).
[8] A.D. Chandler & H. Chandler, *Scale and Scope: The Dynamics of Industrial Capitalism* (1990).
[9] W. Lazonick, *Business Organization and the Myth of the Market* (1991).
[10] A. Amsden, *The Next Asian Giant* (1990).

conditions already were being implemented in the government's emergency program. Negative real money growth and a fiscal surplus of 0.5 percent for 1995 now are included in this strict conditionality, but others are quite new and imply the surveillance of the U.S. Treasury over basic macroeconomic policies in Mexico for the duration of the agreement. Most important, Mexico's obligations to the United States under the agreement are fully backed by the proceeds from Mexico's crude oil and oil products exports. Payments for these exports will pass through an account of the Banco de México at the Federal Reserve Bank of New York; in the case of default, Mexico's obligations will be set off against funds passing through the account.

As a result of these policies, the Mexican economy is being driven into a deep recession. The outlook for 1995 is a negative rate of growth of -5 percent, more than 1.2 million lost jobs, 50 percent inflation and an explosion in the non-performing portfolio of private banks (which grew from 14 million pesos in December 1994 to US$100 million in July 1995). The trade balance will show a surplus (possibly US$2 billion), while the current account balance will still show a deficit of possibly US$5 billion. The total external debt of Mexico will surpass the US$165 billion figure and interest payments will be of the order of US$12 billion.

Most important, the productive capacity of Mexico will have been severely affected by the crisis. If the model was not able to establish adequate linkages between the export sector with the rest of the economy, today the situation is worsened because of the number of firms going out of business. It is not at all clear how the Mexican economy will recover from this crisis and its contractionist medicine. It is possible that when all the dust settles down, we will discover a maimed economy which is not able to grow at rates higher than 3 percent, an unsatisfactory pace by all accounts. A change in the economic strategy to avoid the crisis and establish a new base for stable development is urgently required.

Chapter Three

MEXICO: FROM EUPHORIA TO SACRIFICE

by Léon Bendesky

Hans Magnus Enzensberger says "Europeans have a genius for historical maso-chism, being masters of self-criticism, skepticism, and pessimism. But this is also their strength." In Mexico we have recently gone through a phase of euphoria concerning the transformation of the country, mainly through a broad program of economic reforms and modernization imposed by the Salinas admin-istration. That short phase ended in a kind of shock when the new government very soon had to call on the population to accept yet another round of sacrifices to cope with the financial crisis that exploded in late December 1994. Since then, a sense of overwhelming skepticism and pessimism has extended throughout the country, very similar to Enzensberger's characterization. Hopefully this will end up strengthening our society, pushing it in the direction of more social participa-tion, access to information, and democracy.

1. MODERNIZATION AND SOCIAL FRAGILITY

During the period of euphoria, the government emphasized economic reform over the political opening of the country. The question was explicitly related to the Soviet Union's experience under Gorbachev -- hence the economy had first to be stabilized and reformed to conform to the new conditions created by the dual process of globalization and regionalization. Political reform would come later. But the postponement of real political reform in Mexico has meant the production of an indigenous version of Hollywood's "Back to the Future." Our latest leap forward has ended in the revealed scenario of social and economic

D. G. Dallmeyer (ed.), Joining Together, Standing Apart: National Identities after NAFTA, 63–72.

fragility.

During the period of euphoria, critical voices were dismissed consistently as coming from people who did not understand what the process really entailed, since the country was firmly on the road to the First World. One of the favorite figures of the official rhetoric was that we were entering the "major leagues." The metaphor was unfortunate indeed since major league baseball was on the verge of a long strike.

The modernizing process was enforced from above as if this goal were one which could be achieved rapidly in a very diverse and unequal society, as Mexico still is today. The situation resembles the classic question posed by Tolstoy when he dismissed historical interpretations based on the projects of great men, while forgetting that history has to do with all those common men and women who live their everyday lives beyond the great projects that somehow are disengaged from the concrete forms of survival of the lot of the population. This is probably the greatest weakness of the Salinas regime; and the issue is far from trivial, since it refers to the basic questions of representation and accountability, which the Mexican democracy still lacks.

The economic crisis of late 1994 brought the euphoria to an end, turning the mood into one of general distrust, spasm on the part of businessmen and government officials, and the imposition of a harsh process of adjustment based fundamentally on a very orthodox austerity program. Austerity and economic restrictions are the only political offer available to the government to cope with the peso devaluation and the ensuing inflation, and it is an active part of the social conflict extending throughout the country. Austerity has become, in fact, a defining character of contemporary capitalism and thus is a real cultural issue, more than just a feature of economic policy making. It is especially devastating in countries with increasing inequalities that pervade the social structure, as is the case of Mexico, which has shown a greater concentration of income and wealth during the last decade.

Mexico is undergoing a deep crisis with at least three components. The first is social, with its main expression in the Indian-led insurrection of Chiapas. The second is manifested in the rigid transition of a very resilient and aging political system into a yet undefined form of workable democracy. The third is an unending state of economic austerity.

2. SOCIAL UNREST

The country was taken by surprise on the first day of 1994 with the news of a rebellion by the Zapatista Army of National Liberation in the southern state of

Chiapas. What seemed quite striking about the uprising was, first the surprise of the event and the capacity of the rebels to take over a city and several towns in the state, and second, the very basic demands made on the government by an organized group of indigenous population. This was especially striking as the country was aiming at a rapid modernization that was, in fact, leaving behind too many people. In spite of the ambitious Solidarity program with which the Salinas administration was replacing the traditional forms of social expenditure and even political organization beyond the official party's structure, it became clear that they had a political intention that precluded attention to the most backward part of the population, mainly in a very impoverished state like Chiapas. Poverty is a very long-standing condition for many Mexicans and, for the Indian population, it is compounded with oppression, discrimination, and lack of opportunities. In Chiapas exist rich concentrations of cattle and coffee production with quasi-feudal conditions of life for the poorest population. In effect, Mexico faces a national identity problem based on racial difference, economic position, and access to power that has been exacerbated by recent economic policies.

The armed confrontation was stopped within a few days, although social and political tensions persist, as indicated by hundreds of deaths, the extended presence of the national army, and the progression of three governors since the conflict began. This is by far a deeper confrontation than the government tries to portray. For example, in a recent declaration by Foreign Relations Secretary Gurria, he described the conflict as a war of ink and internet more than a military affair, given the ability of the insurrection leader "Marcos" to penetrate the media.

The insurrection affected both society and the government. A stalemate was created while some effective forms of negotiation were being sought throughout 1994. That never happened, and the conflict, while passive, was in reality aggravated as the Salinas government waited to pass on the conflict in the transition to a new administration. President Zedillo constantly expressed his will to negotiate; yet his actions were contradictory. He changed the official position, showed some hesitation, finally set the national army and the federal policy against the Zapatistas, and began an offensive against dissidents with no direct relations with the rebel groups. Then, just a couple of days later, the government called for the resumption of the negotiations thus sending very mixed political signals. Negotiations are underway still and are expected to last a long time.

3. POLITICAL RESISTANCE

On August 21, 1994, everything seemed well within the ruling party. The Partido Revolucionario Institucional (PRI) was able to recover from the assassination of its presidential candidate. Ernesto Zedillo, a replacement candidate handpicked by President Salinas, won 52 percent of the popular vote in what was the most closely observed election in the country. The mood within the government was one of success, of certainty in its ability to follow the economic program of the outgoing administration, and of confidence in the renewal of the party's strength, which was to continue until the arrival of the 21st century, a feat of constant rule for over 70 years. The PRI seems to be the true example of the permanent revolution, beyond any expectations of the early Bolshevik regime.

But even with these favorable electoral results, the Mexican political environment is becoming increasingly tense. In the first place, the electoral process at the base of the democratic regime is constantly under question. The electoral control of the PRI has weakened, and the Partido Acción Nacional (PAN), an old conservative force, has been making significant gains in congressional and gubernatorial races. Elections have thus become a significant factor in the country's political life. Several reforms had been enacted since the contested elections of 1988 when Salinas became president. At that time the computing system failed and results were postponed for several more days in what was taken as an obvious manipulation of the popular vote by the government. It was only because of the authoritarian political system and the huge power of the presidency that Salinas was able to re-create the rule of the regime and his own position in the executive office. This situation forced the opposition leader, Cuauhtemoc Cardenas, to a strategy of denouncing the legitimacy of the elections, a situation that soon faced its own political limits. Along with constant attacks by the government, including the physical elimination of many of its leaders around the country, the Partido de la Revolucion Democratica (PRD) lost several of its positions during the congressional elections of 1991.

For the 1994 elections the Federal Electoral Institute still operated under the direct control of the Secretária de Gobernacion (Ministry of Interior), but the governing council included six citizen counselors proposed by the political parties and ratified by Congress. This mechanism increased public confidence in the electoral process and its official results, but this public perception was due also to the wide participation of social organizations in observation of the elections. These organizations effectively mobilized scarce human, financial, and technical resources, which included the presence of foreign observers in different parts of the country. The political campaigns and the results of the election still showed the existence of huge irregularities, especially in the use of funds and other resources by the PRI in the unconditional support that it received from most of the media, and also in the corporate control of the vote in many rural areas. In general terms the result of the election was uncontested and Zedillo took office on December 1. But the Mexican democracy is a different sort of phenomenon than that usually understood in advanced industrial countries. The creation of a truly modern social structure depends crucially on the establishment of a democratic regime. Society at large demands a change in the political organization and in the exercise of power.

The ruling PRI is paying dearly for its own political success and long survival. The postponement of effective political reform now has put the party in an awkward position, facing very limited degrees of action and a severe loss of credibility. Party members are suspected of having ordered within a period of six months the assassinations of both Colosio, its original presidential candidate, and Ruiz Massieu, its general secretary, and also of being directly involved in the rapidly increasing drug business, in addition to the well-known wide corruption that plagues the bureaucracy and the political system. But resistance within the party is very strong, and diverse sectors, among them the old guard (the so-called "dinosaurs"), are striving to maintain their respective shares of power and influence at the federal, regional, and local levels. A significant part of the political struggle that takes place in the country takes place within the PRI.

This political decomposition also has led to a weakening of the legal framework in the country. The rule of law is a scarce resource in Mexican society. There is no effective separation of the executive from the legislative and judicial powers; procuration of justice is not only slow but corrupt. Recently, for instance, a group of citizens opposed the location of the judicial police in their neighborhood, thus showing the fear and distrust of society in the institutions that should be providing for individual and collective security. Montesquieu undoubtedly would not be able to live in Mexico, or maybe he would find it an ideal place to test his vision of society, especially the one derived from the spirit of the laws.

Zedillo's presidential campaign was conducted under two main slogans; the first promised "welfare for the family," and the second offered "peace" for the country, in a direct reference to the armed insurrection in the state of Chiapas. Despite the slow economic growth of the past decade (gross domestic product (GDP) increased only by a yearly average of 1.5 percent and real wages showed just a slight increase while total employment was lagging), and the evidence of social contradictions exacerbated by so-called neoliberal policies, many Mexicans believed in these promises, mainly out of fear that the social stability of the country might be further at risk should any other party come into power. "Better bad but known," a popular saying goes. And in fact, according to official propaganda and the huge support given to the PRI by the business sector (especially the bankers who were handsomely rewarded during the Salinas administration), the crisis that now plagues the country should have happened if the left wing PRD had won the election. This position was held explicitly by Roberto Hernandez, head of Banamex, Mexico's large bank.

4. ECONOMIC AUSTERITY

The triumphant mood generated by the elections was truly ephemeral: it lasted less than three weeks after the inauguration of Zedillo's administration. On inauguration day, when he placed the tricolor band around his chest, the new tenant of Los Pinos offered the Mexican people the continuation of his predecessor's economic policies, whom he praised for the reforms instrumented and for the handling of public affairs during his term in office. But on December 19, Secretary of Hacienda (Finance) Serra announced that, due to the pressures on the value of the currency, there was an urgency to adopt a "technical measure:" forcing the young government to expand the band of fluctuation of the exchange rate of the new peso against the U.S. dollar. He explained this did not amount to a devaluation, but in fact, in the course of same day, everybody knew the peso had started a huge depreciation against the dollar, although nobody knew at that time how invasive this process would be and how deep a crisis would be incited.

The behavior of the economy during the second half of Salinas' *sexenio* showed the accumulation of a large current account deficit that was being financed through the entry of foreign capital, mainly portfolio investments placed in government debt instruments. The exchange rate, which had played a crucial role in the government's economic program by acting as a nominal anchor for the rest of the macroeconomic variables, showed greater signs of weakness during 1994, given the degree of over-valuation. Thus, the dollar became one of the least expensive items in the economy. The pre-announced rate of depreciation of the peso against the dollar served, for several years, to attract foreign savings by guaranteeing a high financial return in dollars, but its efficiency came abruptly to an end.

External events played a role in this process, mainly through the increasing political risks perceived by institutional investors. But the crisis has an inherent source that stems from the rigid productive structure of the Mexican economy and its huge sectoral imbalances. This is a fact that government officials were not, and still are not, prepared to accept, claiming instead that a structural transformation was provoked on the economy by the program of reforms that requires only the correct relationship of relative prices to operate efficiently and to support growth mainly through exports. Even though there were voices criticizing the reform, particularly the capacity to sustain the financing of the economy with foreign capital flows, the government maintained its position. There was no hint whatever from the monetary authorities that a foreign exchange crisis was in the making. Salinas rendered his last *Informe* to Congress on 1 November 1994, and asserted his exchange rate policy, as did Zedillo in his inaugural speech. This has given rise to an increasing round of questions concerning the technical and political handling of the devaluation of the peso that cost the head of the Secretary of Finance.

Several calculations placed the level of overvaluation of the peso at around 16 percent which meant that it should have been adjusted from a price of 3.50 per dollar to 4.10. Instead the devaluation sent the peso to a level of 7 per dollar; later it has been stabilized in a zone of around 6 per dollar, which constitutes but one measure of the cost of the crisis. The announcement of the *de facto* devaluation took society by surprise and the immediate crisis which ensued generated social discontent and distrust on the new administration. Skepticism of the government's actions is widespread, but the capacity to react is indeed very unequal. As a result, the way in which the peso crisis was handled allowed a very small group to purchase a large amount of the international reserves at the Bank of Mexico (the Central Bank) in what resulted in a huge plundering of the nation's resources. After that, the depreciation of the peso was unstoppable. This is the way in which a fragile, open economy responded to the needs of global capital in an era of wide financial speculation. The event also showed the symbiosis between government and big capital, a relation concentrated on a new powerful group of entrepreneurs which was created in the recent process of economic reforms and privatization in the country.

The scarcity of monetary reserves expressed itself in a foreign debt crisis, when the payment of the dollar-denominated *Tesobonos*, issued extensively by the government to attract foreign capital since early 1994, was coming to term. This precipitated the negotiations with the United States government for a financial rescue package that, in addition to its economic costs, meant a further political weakening for Zedillo and his cabinet. The final package, that eluded the approval of the U.S. Congress, was realized by the executive power of President Clinton. It is directed solely to address the maturity of *Tesobonos* during the year. Not a single dollar is for use in productive investment. Thus the Mexican government is avoiding an external moratorium, but meanwhile, the domestic economy faces a deep recession and an extensive incapacity to validate current debts. This has created the necessity of a large government intervention in financial markets and banking institutions in yet another reaction against liberalization policies implemented in that sector of the economy.

Zedillo had offered a period of growth and well-being based on the same economic policies instrumented by Salinas, but very rapidly the expected evolution of the economy for 1995 has been worsening in a process that shows the inability of the government to apply measures to contain the crisis. The situation has been complicated by delayed and conflicting technical measures, while the economy deteriorates and the political support for the government weakens.

The original budget for 1995, presented to Congress even before the new President took office, assumed 3.2 percent increase of GDP, an inflation rate of 7 percent, a current account deficit of US$213.4 billion, with an exchange rate of 4.05 pesos per dollar and an average nominal interbank interest rate around 17 percent. Instead, the first revision of the macroeconomic goals announced in early January 1995 offered a GDP rate of increase of 1.5 percent, an inflation of 19.5 percent, a current account deficit of US$14 billion, and an exchange rate of 4.50 pesos per dollar. This revision was very quickly surpassed as the economic situation deteriorated rapidly. Thus, the latest program presented in March 1995 called instead for a reduction of GDP of 2 percent, an inflation rate of 42 percent, and a current account deficit of US$2 billion, while interest rates have risen above 100 percent per year and are currently around 70 percent. The economic conditions have a clear anti-productive bias and private sources are expecting a reduction in GDP on the order of -4 percent and an inflation rate of 55 percent. The credit squeeze is causing a severe restriction of aggregate demand in order to control inflation pressures, but at the expense of production and employment in the midst of increasing social demands for income-generating activities.

The adjustment program instrumented by the government is rigorously restrictive in its attempt to stabilize the economy; it is a most orthodox policy that projects a fiscal surplus of 4.4 percent of GDP in an economy that is in a state of virtual paralysis. Fiscal policy is targeted to the increase in government revenues through the rise in taxes (especially value-added tax (VAT)) and the prices of public goods, mainly energy, while expenditures in public investment are falling radically and interest payments on public debt is growing at a very rapid rate. The main instrument to restrict aggregate demand in the economy is monetary policy, which is extremely tight. There is not even a hint of applying supply policies to maintain the level of economic activity. Unemployment is rising at a very rapid rate and is expected to reach two million people out of work during 1995 in a country where a million new workers enter the labor market every year. The labor ministry estimates six million people out of work just four months after the start of the crisis. As consequence, incomes are dropping rapidly in what everybody understands as a situation where the working population, the middle classes, and small and medium firms are clearly the victims. The government first declared that during the second half of 1995 the economy could show some recovery, but now it is expecting still harsher conditions well into the end of the year.

5. CHANGED NATIONAL SCENARIO

The fixation with balanced macroeconomic accounts which currently pervades economic thought and policy making is becoming a perverse social policy, and it is increasing the cost of the crisis. There is open risk of a social fracture in the country. Discontent with the sudden change in the economic scenario and the erratic actions of the administration is growing very fast among businessmen and the population at large, as shown in the reactions against the recent acceptance by Congress of the 50 percent increase in the value-added tax. The PRI majority in both the Chambers of Deputies and Senators voted in favor of the tax hike in an act that confirms the complete dependence of the legislative power on the executive in what is known as the system of the *PRI-gobierno*.

The economic crisis erupted as a run on the peso, but its financial impact is just the immediate expression of the dual process of rising political instability that started in late 1993 and of the endemic structural problems of the Mexican economy. What is surprising is not the emergence of the crisis, but the way the government handled the economic situation and applied the adjustment measures. The economic scenario and the state of expectations in the country changed 180 degrees, not only in relation to the image provided by the previous administration, but also in relation to the offer of the new one which was maintained until the very outburst of the crisis.

The strategy of economic reforms instrumented in the country during the last decade was directed to the opening of trade and financial flows, the liberalization of markets (with the significant exception of wages and for a long time the exchange rate), and the change in property rights. But it did not contain the necessary complementary policies to achieve the desired objectives and reduce the intrinsic vulnerability of the productive structure and the fragility of the financial sector. Economic policy was conducted under a very limited perspective that gave privilege to monetary and international issues, and left behind crucial institutional aspects of the organization of the economy and society as well as the existing internal and external relations of power. Long-delayed political reform has created greater conflicts that now exacerbate the confrontation between the state and the political parties and other social organizations. With the transition to a democratic regime becoming an ever wider social demand, Zedillo's offer to restructure the balance of powers in the country needs effective actions to gain credibility. A political solution to the insurrection in Chiapas still hangs on his ability to effectively lead the country. The unsolved crimes of political figures and the continuous corruption scandals are creating a moral crisis. The economic conditions are drastically shortening the horizon for the majority of the population. In the meantime, the government is being increasingly isolated, with adverse repercussions on the political unity of the nation.

Chapter Four

NAFTA, QUEBEC, AND THE BOUNDARIES OF CULTURAL SOVEREIGNTY: THE CHALLENGE OF IDENTITY IN THE ERA OF GLOBALIZATION

by Daniel Salée

Canadian critics of free trade agreements with the United States have often expressed their concerns over the consequences such agreements will have on Canada's cultural sovereignty. Even before the Free Trade Agreement (FTA) and North American Free Trade Agreement (NAFTA) were struck, they argue, Canadian cultural industries were already largely controlled by American interests and submitted to the United States policy agenda; with those trade deals, Canada has finally capitulated. Referring to the FTA, Mel Hurtig wrote:

> The agreement freezes Canadian cultural policy in place. In what was trumpeted as a great victory for Canada, the Mulroney government has effectively agreed that the heavy U.S. dominance of Canada's cultural industries would be forever written in stone as part of the agreement and that any important future attempt to implement Canadian cultural initiatives would have to be approved first in Washington.[1]

For Maude Barlow and Bruce Campbell, the gravest consequence of this state of affairs for Canada is that "when our cultural voice goes, our independent, critical, political voice is silenced as well. [Free trade agreements are] cutting the vocal chords [sic] of dissent. . . . The result, for Canada, is a country reshaped to fit George Bush's new world order."[2]

---

[1]   M. Hurtig, *The Betrayal of Canada* 189 (1991).
[2]   M. Barlow & B. Campbell, *Take Back the Nation* 108-109 (1991).

D. G. Dallmeyer (ed.), Joining Together, Standing Apart: National Identities after NAFTA, 73–89.

Interestingly, insofar as Quebec is concerned, the issue is easily dealt with: cultural sovereignty in the context of a continent-wide trade bloc is simply not a problem that seems to be haunting Quebecers, at least not in the official discourse of most private and public decision makers. There has always been a fairly wide consensus among the Quebec population about the benefits of free trade for the economic and social development of the province. The November 1988 federal general election, which was largely fought on the issue of the Free Trade Agreement, is usually seen as a key indicator of this consensus. Quebecers largely contributed to keep the Mulroney government in power by electing 63 Conservative, pro-free trade members of Parliament (MPs) out of the 75 representing the province of Quebec in Parliament. Since the early 1980s, the idea of a free-trade zone between Canada and the United States has always had a significant appeal in Quebec, especially among the emerging francophone business élite and most government officials dealing with economic development and trade issues. Economic advisers and the powers that be within both the *Parti Québécois* and the Liberal Party have restlessly pushed the idea of free-trade forward, though from somewhat different perspectives and for different reasons.[3] Even the labour movement, despite its original critical disapproval, has come on side; though still not overly enthusiastic about the concept, it more or less considers it now as a "necessary ill."

By and large, Quebecers do not share the reticence of their English Canadian counterparts *vis-à-vis* free trade. The fears and worries of left-nationalist English Canadians that free trade tolls the bell of Canadian cultural sovereignty and distinctiveness, and increases the dependency of the Canadian policy agenda on that of the United States,[4] have as yet little, and in some milieux, no resonance in Quebec. On the contrary, there is a fairly well-entrenched sense in Quebec that free trade is exactly what the province's economy needs. Indeed, Quebec proponents of free trade point approvingly to the constant increases in Quebec exports to the United States and the general strengthening of Quebec as a trading partner.[5] Many among them also think that the economic benefits of free trade

---

[3]   Martin, "Free Trade and Party Politics in Quebec," in C.F. Doran & G.P. Marchildon (eds.), *The NAFTA Puzzle: Political Parties and Trade in North America* 143-171 (1994).

[4]   *See* Bartow & Campbell, *supra* note 2; Hurtig, *supra* note 1; P. Resnick, *Letter to a Québécois Friend* (1990); Watkins, *Madness and Ruin: Politics and the Economy in the Neoconservative Age* (1992).

[5]   G. Lachapelle, *Quebec Under Free Trade: Between Sovereignty and Economic Integration* (paper presented at the ninth biennial conference of the American Council for Quebec Studies, Washington, D.C., 1994); Bakris, "Free Trade in North America: Divergent Perspectives Between Quebec and English Canada," 16 *Quebec Stud.* 39-48 (1993); Latouche, "Quebec in the Emerging North American Configuration," in R. Earle & J. Wirth

can only enhance Quebec's self-affirmation, and eventually guarantee its political sovereignty. Free trade is seen as a means to emancipate the province from English Canadian economic control, a goal openly and avowedly pursued since the 1960s by every government in Quebec City.

The issue of cultural sovereignty with respect to free trade is one that is hardly ever addressed in Quebec. This does not mean that the collective cultural identity of Quebecers is not an issue; it is, in fact, shot through the political landscape of Quebec, practically since the Conquest of New France by England in 1760.[6] Simply, the existence since the mid-1970s of strong, protective language legislation provides a heightened sense of security and confidence in the preservation of the province's distinctiveness. Despite the fantastic pull of American norms and values, language laws are often said to prevent Quebecers from total absorption into the more global, more powerful vortex of American culture.[7] In addition, as the expression of Quebec nationalism progressively moved from essentially ethnocultural terms of reference to more economic ones, it became quite clear to most people concerned by the question that nationalism did not have to imply isolationism.[8] Today, Quebec nationalism is pluralistic and largely open to the world.[9]

Paradoxically, in recent years, the whole question of Quebec's cultural sovereignty in the face of North American integration has been taken up by English-speaking Canadians. Drawing on George Grant's masterful critique of the influence of U.S. civilization on Canadian civic culture,[10] and projecting their own fear and distrust of American cultural imperialism on Quebec, they warn Quebecers against the dangers of acculturation.[11] In their view, independence or any institutional arrangement aimed at consolidating Quebec's political autonomy from the rest of Canada can only make Quebec weaker and unable to resist the assault of U.S. cultural dictates.

(eds.), *Identities in North America: The Search for Community* 117-139 (1995); Holland, "Quebec's Successful Role and Champion of North American Free Trade," 19 *Quebec Stud*. 71-84 (1995).

[6] C. Dufour, *Le défi québécois* (1989).

[7] Morin, Preface to G. Grant, *Est-ce la fin du Canada?* ix-xxi (1988) (trans. from English by Gaston Laurion); Thomas, George Grant, "The Free Trade Agreement, and Contemporary Quebec," 27 *J. Canadian Stud*. 180-196 (no. 4 1993).

[8] Martin, "When Nationalism Meets Continentalism: The Politics of Free Trade in Quebec," 5 *J. Regional & Fed. Stud*. 1-27 (no. 1, 1995).

[9] Balthazar, "L'évolution du nationalisme québécois," in Daigle, Gérard, & Rocher (eds.), *Le Québec en jeu* 647-666 (1992).

[10] G. Grant, *Lament for a Nation* (1965).

[11] *See* Resnick, *supra* note 4; Thomas, *supra* note 7.

Though well intended, their warning is fraught with misunderstanding about the nature of culture and cultural change. The expressions thought to be typical of a given culture are not static. Cultural manifestations reflect the internal dynamic of a society; a culture is a process of social relations. Depending on the conjuncture and the nature of its evolution, a culture may well become at ease with new paradigms that in an earlier epoch it would have completely rejected. When the exponents of a particular culture come to adopt the terms, norms, and values of a culture that is exogenous to theirs, it does not necessarily mean that they have given up on their own culture; it simply means that they have re-tooled the terms and parameters of their identity. They may, in fact, express their identity more forcefully and more productively with a new discourse, however borrowed it may be from another stronger, dominant culture. They use the language of that culture to state the case for the preservation of their identity more cogently.

Given the somewhat paternalistic undertones of the warnings of English Canadian cultural doomsayers, it is hard not to think that they are somehow still caught in a pre-modern vision of Quebec culture which, it seems, they would like to see preserved. It was, of course, a much less threatening culture to English Canada; a culture of submissiveness and self-centered isolation which successfully kept French-speaking Quebecers in silent acceptance of their second-class status within the Canadian federation.

The fact of the matter is, though, both the confident Quebec nationalists and their English Canadian detractors miss the point when considering the implications and consequences of NAFTA for Quebec's cultural sovereignty. Sovereignty is, in many ways, an elastic notion. We give it the content that corresponds to what the particular goals of citizenship at a given juncture dictate. Sovereignty is a socially and politically determined construct entirely submitted to the vagaries of history and social struggles. While one generation, class, or social group may be perfectly happy with particular boundaries of sovereignty, others will not, on account of differing social, political, or economic agendas.

The point of the whole issue of cultural sovereignty with respect to NAFTA rests on a question of larger proportion and import. NAFTA is simply the North American expression of the irresistible process of globalization that is determining the social and economic configuration of most nations around the world. In this respect, then, the fundamental question that must be raised is: what are the consequences of globalization on the cultural parameters and identity of modern Quebec? As globalization pushes local economies and societies into openness to the outside world, as it brings down the traditional boundaries of sovereignty, how can a society like Quebec define a collective project of its own, in tune with the requirements of its historical evolution?

Such questions, in fact, constitute the crux of the matter with regard to cultural sovereignty in the wake of NAFTA. The consequences of NAFTA on Quebec's cultural make-up are broader in their implications than considerations about Quebec's ability to protect its boundaries from cultural imperialism, or avert breaches to the province's cultural integrity. The real issue at hand is whether or not Quebec can and will remain Quebec and preserve its particular identity: is the sociocultural project articulated by Quebec sovereignists and nationalists over the past three decades still feasible within a wider, globalizing context of continental integration?

Before I can address this question, it is necessary to grasp fully the significance of globalization. Sociologist Roland Robertson put it succinctly:

> [T]he global field as a whole is a sociocultural 'system' which has resulted from the compression of -- to the point that it increasingly imposes constraints upon, but also differentially empowers -- civilizational cultures, national societies, intra- and cross-national movements and organizations, sub-societies and ethnic groups, intra-societal quasi-groups and so on. As the general process of globalization proceeds there is a concomitant constraint upon such entities to 'identify' themselves in relations to the global-human circumstance. . . . [G]lobalization has involved and continues to involve the *institutionalized construction* of the individual. Even more specifically, we must recognize that world-political culture has led to globewide institutionalization of the 'life course' -- which has two dimensions: aspects of the person that enter into rationalized social organization and the public celebration of the 'private' or subjective individual.[12]

Clearly, Robertson is in fact pointing to "the decomposition and the loss of a hitherto functioning civic myth," the polymorphous offering on the public place of "contending visions of political community."[13] As tribalism seems to gain new grounds through manifestations as extreme as ethnic cleansing in former Yugoslavia and the tragic, mind-boggling massacres in Rwanda -- but also through the less spectacular, though no less lethal, everyday, insidious expressions of intolerance and exclusivism in the so-called advanced societies -- many feel we are losing the sense of civic commonality which keeps members of modern societies rallied around undisputed cultural and state boundaries, beyond the parochialism and narrowness of their own specific identity. The question is why are growing segments of liberal-democratic societies now prepared to tread the path of limited identities?

Fifty years ago, in a little-known article, economic historian and social

[12] R. Robertson, *Globalization: Social Theory and Global Culture* 61, 104-105 (1992).
[13] Maier, "Democracy and its Discontents," 73 *Foreign Aff.* 48-64, 57, 60 (no. 4, 1994).

thinker Karl Polanyi observed from the vantage point of his own epoch that in the wake of "the simultaneous downfall of liberal capitalism, world-revolutionary socialism and racial domination -- the three competing forms of universalist societies -- . . . three various forms of inherently limited existence emerge[d] -- new forms of socialism, of capitalism, of planned and semi-planned economies -- each of them, by their very nature, *regional.*"[14] Although Polanyi was referring to economic realities, his observation brings to light the eminently particularistic dynamic that generally echoes periods of universalistic socioeconomic processes. Indeed, in the history of humanity, parochial tendencies -- some call them tribalism -- have often developed in times of social and economic restructuring, in times when it seemed one could no longer take for granted the foundations of cultural and social existence to which one was accustomed. We are now experiencing such a time.[15]

Business and political leaders extol the virtues of globalization. They revel in the great competitive challenges, the extended markets, and the promising prospects of economic growth that it seems to entail. They are rather silent, however, about the actual repercussions of globalization: plant closures and higher unemployment on account of economic rationalization, displacement of human resources, dislocation of communities, annihilation of peripheral cultures have become all-too-familiar stories for an ever-growing number of people.

In the West, globalization is bringing about the final breakdown of the postwar social contract. We have now come to take as normal rates of unemployment in excess of 10 percent and we exhort the state to stop fending for those who fall by the wayside. Outside the advanced capitalist world, globalization is bringing marginal economies to irreversible bankruptcy and is reinforcing the process of deculturation undertaken under colonialism.

Regardless of the format it takes, the result is the same everywhere. The steamrolling and homogenizing market forces extant in the process of globalization have triggered a deep-rooted crisis of identity. The imperatives of economic restructuring and the often forced adaptation of national economies to the dictates of international markets are rendering obsolete and irrelevant familiar parameters of social and cultural identity. As the sociocultural universe in which the personal existence of individuals is anchored crumbles, distrust and suspicion of otherness naturally take center stage. Alterity becomes a threat. People tend to

---

[14]   Polanyi, "Universal Capitalism or Regional Planning?" *London Q. World Aff.* 86-91, 86 (Jan. 1945).

[15]   M. Horsman & A. Marshall, *After the Nation-State: Citizens, Tribalism and the New World Disorder* (1994).

retreat into the world they know and like, and they try to maintain or re-create it in as pure a form as possible. That is the pattern followed by ethnonationalist movements, religious fundamentalist groups, and political essentialists. But it is a pattern that is also found among most groups or social classes which stand to lose power, sociopolitical prominence, or simply a way of life to which they cling.

This re-creation of crumbling worlds leads to the tragic search for scape-goats. They are generally religious, ethnic, racial, or cultural groups other than one's own; they are the poor, the destitute, women, and all those who are forced to exist at the margins of society. Ethnic cleansing and other such ugly manifes-tations of tribalism reflect this tragic search.

Supporters of economic restructuring and globalization often dismiss particularistic political agendas as purportedly out of tune with the irresistible and evolving exigencies of modernity: to resist globalization by asserting and defending parochial sociopolitical or economic goals is to stand in the way of progress -- essentially, economic progress. Such a view is impervious to the sociocultural dimensions of globalization. Indeed, through the sociocultural looking glass, globalization takes a texture quite different from that which the economic and homogeneic understanding of it bears out. In spite of its homogen-izing pull, globalization is not without producing a societal framework of differ-entiation and valorization of particular identities. Reacting to homogenization, particularistic, national, social, economic, and cultural identities strive hard for recognition and strongly assert their specificity in the face of the globalizing process.

Globalization has instituted within contemporary societies a social dynamic which, far from subordinating the subject to a universalistic whole, results in its actual, albeit unintended, glorification. The consequences of this are felt in the attendant fragmentation of the sociopolitical fabric woven by modernity as a multitude of particular, limited, and local identities are seeking to create singular spheres of autonomy with which to stake their claims on the body politic.[16] To-day's social interactions are, therefore, inevitably trapped in the tension between cultural homogenization and cultural heterogenization.[17] The tribalistic pull so decried by many bears the imprint of this tension.

It is against the backdrop of this particular outcome of globalization that one

---

[16] Freitag, "L'identité, l'altérité et le politique. Essai exploratoire de reconstruction con-ceptuelle-historique," 9 *Société* 1-55 (1992); G. Lipovetsky, *L'ère du vide*, coll. Folio essais (1983).
[17] Appadurai, "Disjuncture and Difference in the Global Cultural Economy," II *Public Culture* 2 (1990).

must try to assess the consequences of NAFTA for cultural sovereignty. The fact of the matter is that globalization triggers a societal dynamic which is likely to alter our sense of political community and the parameters of citizenship that we are prepared to tolerate. Globalization affects the internal sociopolitical logic of national societies in ways that we have yet to understand. The real impact of NAFTA, and therefore of globalization, is not going to be felt in terms of immediate, formal changes to the structural, legal, and territorial boundaries of our national states. National states are simply going to move closer to each other, closer to a unitary and more totalizing vision of governance which cuts across national territorial borders.

The real impact of globalization is going to be felt in terms of the way members of national political communities react to the process of globalization as they are affected by it. That is why it is virtually pointless to talk of cultural sovereignty as though the whole issue could simply be discussed in terms of a mere battle of ideological, intellectual, or moral influence between territorially sovereign states. It is pointless because the societal reaction to globalization will, in time, amount to nothing less than a full-fledged cultural revolution against the homogenizing, integrating, centralizing, and universalistic models inherent in and borne out by the process of globalization.

Globalization is the latest stage of a long, civilizational process started roughly 500 years ago: a process premised on the transcendental imperatives of liberal-democratic reason, a totalizing and Euro-centric conception of human societies, and the triumph of the Western view of the world. Like most processes, however, Western civilization contains the seeds of its own contradiction. Today, pushing the model to the outer limits of its liberal-democratic logic, social movements armed with the discourse of individual and civil rights are turning the process -- or more precisely the results of the process -- on its head. They are demanding nothing less than the reconfiguration of the public sphere, suggesting new criteria of governance, propounding a politics of identity and difference, celebrating all manners of heterogeneous, polymorphous, and hybrid societal models, which, perforce, negate the universalistic assumptions upon which modern society is predicated.[18]

This emerging context of new social relations and re-patterned political interaction directly affects the exercise of sovereignty within the modern state. For a long time, the territorial boundaries of sovereign states were coterminous with a clearly circumscribed national market. Those who used and controlled the national market were generally happy with the geographic limits within which it

[18]   A. Yeatman, *Postmodern Revisionings of the Political* (1994).

operated and conducted their business strictly within those limits. Since the beginning of the 20th century, domestic markets have become largely insufficient for the further development and reproduction of capitalism in most Western industrial societies. This first led to the internationalization of capital and the multinationalization of domestic economies -- a dual process which accelerated considerably after World War II -- and eventually to a greater degree of cultural homogeneity across territorial boundaries, thanks to the concomitant progress of communication technologies.

Today, McLuhan's global village trivializes the geographic and political borders on the basis of which the will to sovereignty traditionally staked its claims. The significance and sanctity of sovereignty are now rather diluted. What does sovereignty mean when a critical article about the Canadian economy in the *Wall Street Journal* and international traders' disinterest for the Canadian dollar trigger panic within Canadian governmental circles and a rise in the Canadian interest rate? How is sovereignty upheld when the information ban of a Canadian judge on a court case is easily bypassed through access to Internet and U.S. newspapers? How is the sovereignty of the Canadian legal culture preserved when students in Canadian law schools learn more about the judicial process and litigation techniques by watching the broadcasts of the O.J. Simpson trial than in their own classrooms?

Globalization, which is itself founded on the relentless drive for market expansion, belittles the will to sovereignty. More importantly, it strikes at the heart of essential principles of sovereignty which hold that the exercise of political authority can only take place within clearly defined territorial boundaries and that the territorial integrity of the modern nation-state is untouchable. International military interventions in intra- and inter-state conflicts, or the extreme dependency of weak national economies upon stronger ones, point to the fact that the traditional conception of sovereignty is for an increasing number of states, much more of moral principle than an actual reality. For all that, the international order still rests, in theory, on the idea of the sovereign state, and around the world a host of national groups without an officially recognized state are striving to obtain one; sovereignty has become a highly relative and elusive goal. For many countries today, state boundaries are merely symbolic.[19]

This withering away of territorially-defined state sovereignty is not without having a direct impact on the exercise of authority within sovereign political

---

[19] Camilleri, "Rethinking Sovereignty in a Shrinking, Fragmented World," in R.B.J. Walker & S. (eds.), *Contending Sovereignties: Redefining Political Communities* 13-44 (1990); Weber, *Simulating Sovereignty: Intervention, the State and Symbolic Exchange* (1995).

spaces. The deconstruction of the traditional boundaries of state sovereignty by the process of globalization is clearing the way for the attendant deconstruction, within national political communities of the hitherto agreed upon postulate, according to which the exercise of authority by the state on own its territory is unlimited, undivisible, and represents the common will. Increasingly, the legitimacy of the state is questioned from inside the society to which it applies. As Joseph Camilleri has noted:

> The postulated coincidence between state sovereignty and a single cohesive community bears little relationship to the known facts. Notwithstanding appeal to nationalism or the national interest, modern societies are deeply fragmented, unable to express the underlying unity that gives public authority its discipline and legitimacy, and on which the claim to sovereignty ultimately rests. . . . What is in question is the legitimacy of the state, the validity of its claim to sovereignty. To this extent the crisis of legitimacy may be interpreted as a crisis of sovereignty, for what is at issue is the nature of the state, the interests it represents, its relationship to civil society. The crisis, which has both theoretical and practical ramifications, is shaped by a period of far-reaching realignment of concepts, allegiances, and institutions. It is a period in which appeals to national interest and national loyalties, though still fashionable in many quarters, are generally losing their capacity to mobilize human energies and material resources.[20]

Canada and Quebec are illustrations of the circumstances described by Camilleri. For five years, between 1987 and 1992, as they navigated often murky waters from the Meech Lake to the Charlottetown Accords, Canadians collectively tried to redesign their constitution, but to no avail. The process collapsed lamentably on the reefs of the 1992 referendum over the Charlottetown Accord. This failure reflected, in fact, the impossibility for Canadians to agree on one common definition or conception of their political community, on one acceptable, unifying vision of their polity. During those five years, myriad voices were heard, but hardly ever converged on mutually agreeable parameters of sociability and conviviality. Each was seeking in this constitutional exercise a means to promote or protect very particularistic agendas, often in defiance of the structures and principles upon which has historically rested the Canadian state.[21]

A similar situation is taking place in Quebec as the republican ideal and civic nationalism upon which the sovereignist project is now said to be predicated[22] is being called into question by the particularistic concerns of various ethnocul-

---

[20]   Camillieri, *supra* note 19, at 37-38.

[21]   Rocher & Salée, "Démocratie et réforme constitutionnelle: discours et pratique," *Int'l J. Canadian Stud./Revue internationale d'études canadiennes*, 167-187 (no. 7, 1993).

[22]   Legaré, "La souveraineté: nation ou raison?" in A.G. Gagnon (ed.), *Quebec: État et société* 41-60 (1994).

tural communities. Under the influence of a strong and broad-based nationalist movement, Quebec has aspired over the past three decades to being recognized as a nation-state on account of its cultural and linguistic distinctiveness. Despite the federal government's constant opposition to the idea of Quebec sovereignty and a certain historical reticence on the part of the Quebec electorate to endorse it wholeheartedly, the current Quebec government is now poised to realize a sociopolitical project unequivocally rooted in the will to create an autonomous public space, a space of political sovereignty that French-speaking Quebecers could truly call their own.

Admittedly, in recent years, the formulators of Quebec nationalism have substantially redefined its traditionally strong ethnic undertones. They now claim that Quebec nationalism must be understood within a broader perspective, that of a civic and territorial nationalism whereby all Quebecers, regardless of their origin and ethnocultural or linguistic difference, would rally around a neutral and democratic state where French would be the common language of public transactions.[23] Notwithstanding the liberal, generous, and inclusionary outlook of Quebec's new nationalism, many sociocultural minority groups and social movements within Quebec are resisting the universalistic but homogenizing project of an independent Quebec state as French-speaking Quebec sovereignists formulate it. In this respect, as a truly modern society, Quebec is facing the exact same predicament to which Camilleri is alluding. Buying into the process of individualization to which Robertson refers, these minority groups and social movement are objecting to Quebec's will to statehood for the same reason Quebec sovereignists have historically taken issue with the structural, legal, and administrative dominion of the Canadian state: they too are claiming a space of autonomy outside the bounds of the state, though this time it is outside the state Quebec sovereignists are trying desperately to build.

The Aboriginal question in Quebec is a case in point.[24] Historically, Quebec's basis of political bargaining within Canada has been founded on the idea of a compact between the two ethnolinguistic communities (French and English) that created the country in 1867. Such an idea implies strict political parity between the two groups. Although the two-founding-nations principle propounded by Quebec was often resisted by English Canadian politicians, it still succeeded over time in securing Quebec a modicum of prominence within the Canadian federation.

---

[23] Parti Québécois, *Quebec in a New World* (1994).

[24] *See* Salée, "Identities in Conflict: The Aboriginal Question and the Politics of Recognition in Quebec," 18 *Ethnic & Racial Studies* 277-314 (1995).

The Constitution Act of 1982 brought an end to this fragile political equilibrium both by obfuscating the notion of the two founding majorities so dear to Quebec, and by promoting a cultural policy founded on constitutional minoritarianism.[25] From then on, Quebec would have much less clout in the Canadian political system than its history had allowed. In the context of the new Constitution, Quebec's particular claims deserved no more special attention than those of other cultural minorities who, henceforth, became invested with their own real constitutional identity. The Charter "reinforces the identities of minorities that have no territorial base other than the Canadian national community in the aggregate," and so the political culture which emanates from it "[removes] all reference to duality, to the notion of two majorities and to that of a distinct political community in Quebec."[26]

In this context, the credibility and the legitimacy of arguments for Quebec identity become weaker in the face of Aboriginal claims, which are themselves based on the predication of a specific identity. In the current Canadian constitutional and legislative framework, one identity is worth as much as another: a hierarchy of identities, as the notion of two founding nations implies, can logically no longer be tolerated. The Aboriginal peoples have understood this well, and that is why some of their leaders did not fear to go as far as to deny the existence of a distinct Quebec people or to challenge Quebec's territorial boundaries.

The Aboriginal position is clear: the Aboriginal right to self-determination is no less important than the desire of Quebecers to control their own national destiny. In the Aboriginal frame of mind, this idea is held as paramount if ever any exercise of redefinition of the social contract, whether at the pan-Canadian level or at the Quebec level, is to go through successfully. Quebec's identity should not in any way take precedence over Aboriginal identity.

The constitutional negation of Quebec's specificity leads then to two points of tension which complicate the dynamic of relations between the Aboriginal and non-Aboriginal peoples of Quebec. First, on the basis of the constitutional logic which currently prevails, the Aboriginals feel justified in questioning the particular identity claims of Quebecers -- they are not alone, either, in feeling so justified, as the opposition from English Canada to the Meech Lake Accord has demonstrated. This is a logical strategy which comes all the more naturally to them since it is the federal state, and not the provincial state, which has been historically their principal interlocutor. On the whole, despite their oft-stated desire to evolve outside the non-Aboriginal institutional machinery, they opt

---

[25]   G. Laforest, *Trudeau et la fin d'un rêve canadien* 189 (1992).
[26]   *Id.* at 190.

ever more willingly for the preservation of the federal political regime. Secondly, by virtue of the dominant constitutional logic, the Aboriginals are equally
justified in pursuing their own identity claims. As these latter seem bound to lead
to territorial reappropriation, they are inevitably construed by French-speaking
Quebecers as a frontal assault against the Quebec identity, whose foundation is
intimately tied to a geographic territoriality that is generally considered by the
Quebec government as inalienable, untouchable, and most of all non-negotiable.

The Aboriginal question might be seen as a somewhat extreme case. Aboriginal nations in Quebec are not all seeking to establish the political primacy of
their own sense of nationhood over or against that of Quebecers. And clearly,
the identity claims of anglophones and immigrants have never entailed the creation of separate constituencies outside Quebec's political and administrative
bounds. Still, the claims made by Aboriginals, anglophones, and immigrants
alike are couched in the varied language of political and administrative autonomy, sociopolitical inclusion, cultural or linguistic leeway, and flexible conditions of citizenship. In this sense, to the extent that Quebec sovereignty appears
to reflect the hegemonic aspirations of the French-speaking majority to Aboriginals, anglophones, and immigrants, it is out of line with the requisite of a democratic and individual rights-oriented society, and thus, in the end, fundamentally
unacceptable. Whether their perception of Quebec nationalism and will to sovereignty is right or ill-advised is immaterial. Politically, Aboriginals, anglophones,
and immigrants constitute a social force of opposition unwilling to heed any
sovereignist call to civic unity or appeal to national interest. To them Quebec
nationalism, even in its new theoretical garb, still bears the imprint of French
Canadian ethnicity. The will to political sovereignty only makes sense as it
applies to "old-stock" Quebecers. Few outside the French-speaking community
feel any allegiance to, or included in, the sociopolitical project of Quebec sovereignists. That is the irremediable bottom line. So long as Quebec sovereignty
will continue to be defined within the traditional parameters of the nation-state,
sovereignists will likely continue to trip on this major stumbling block.

In fact, some representatives of ethnocultural communities go as far as to call
for a complete, conceptual overhaul of the *Québécois* identity. Their own blue-
print for the future of Quebec society is largely at odds with what sovereignists
have in mind and includes transculturality and *métissage* as the cornerstones of
that overhaul. They object to the fact that the francophone view of the world has
come to take so much prominence in Quebec's process of self-redefinition. Quebec's *projet collectif*, they feel, must break free from the reminiscences of a
history that large segments of the population have not experienced. Quebec's
new clothes cannot be sewn with the fabric of the past. They believe the

foundational myths which inspire sovereignists to be untenable and out of touch with the increasingly heterogeneous constitutive reality of Quebec society. Quebec must be reconstructed on a new basis that should exclude any hierarchy of group identities and other monopolistic claims by one constituency over the sociocultural content of the society Quebecers are trying to build.[27] This will to redefine the Quebec political community according to entirely new criteria of conviviality and social interaction is predicated upon the desire to formulate an identity for Quebec that, in the end, really has little to do with *Québécois's* historical aspirations as the province's political leadership and intellectual elite understand them.

In essence, I have argued so far that sovereignty in the traditional, narrow sense of the word is an impossible objective to achieve in the current context of integration. Hence, the whole issue of cultural sovereignty with respect to the impact of NAFTA on Quebec (and Canada) is a false problem, for unless the broadcasting of American television, the distribution of American movies, the sale of American popular magazines, and Internet were banned in Canada and Quebec, there is very little chance that a typical, unadulterated, Canadian and *Québécois* culture or even sense of self can ever be properly protected and developed. NAFTA irremediably consecrates the final integration of Canadian and Quebec cultures into the realm of American civilization. Only those with a static conception of culture, who cling to a vision frozen at a particular point in time of the cultural configuration of a society, will despair at this perspective. Given the largely symbolic character of sovereignty nowadays, it is too late for such lament.

The real significance of NAFTA for the cultural sovereignty of Quebec (and Canada) lies elsewhere. It manifests itself in terms far different than what is normally entailed by the idea of sovereignty (i.e. the protection and maintenance of the territorial and sociocultural integrity of the modern nation-state). Largely because of globalization, because of the inherent logic of heightened competition implied by it, instead of seeking a common ground for the reconstitution of the body politic, members of modern societies are seeking to create their own spaces of social interaction which they long to pattern according to the specificities of their particular agenda, even to the detriment of others, if need be. From a strictly cultural perspective -- culture being understood here in its broad, anthropological sense -- that is the fundamental consequence with which we have yet to grapple in the wake of NAFTA.

---

[27]   Tassinari, "La ville continue. Montréal et l'expérience transculturelle de *Vice Versa*," 21/61 *Revue internationale d'action communautaire* 57-62 (1989).

It would be exaggerated to blame directly on NAFTA the emergence of the divide discussed above between the proponents of Quebec sovereignty and those who reject its underlying narrative and sociopolitical project. Nevertheless, to the extent that this situation is born out of the globalizing process, of which NAFTA is but a concrete manifestation, this divide exemplifies the challenge posed to both sovereignty and cultural integrity by the globalizing tendency of modernity: are these still valid political objectives?

Clearly, the process of identity celebration brought about by globalization implies the emergence of a political dynamic questioning the homogenizing drive of sovereignists. In this sense, Quebec sovereignists are facing the dilemma that all other modern societies are facing today: can a wholly pluralistic, fully inclusionary conception of citizenship be applied to modern political communities? It is a tall order. So long as sovereignty entails a totalizing will to subsume difference into a general, unified and centralized framework of sociopolitical interaction (the nation-state), sovereignists will painfully find themselves at odds with the growing and irreversible heterogeneity of the current social fabric of modern Quebec, however de-ethnicized their discourse has become in recent years. The most important challenge the *Parti Québécois* has to face is to prove that its will to become a nation-state does not imply the eventual negation in the public place of ethnocultural expressions other than the French. It will literally have to create a new ethics of intercultural relations and construct a truly open, accepting, and accommodating multicultural society. It will have to do so both to demonstrate that its sociopolitical project transcends narrow ambitions of ethnic empowerment and to show the world that a new, sovereign Quebec state rightly and deservedly belongs in the ranks of modern advanced democratic countries.

That may be easier said than done. Although French-speaking Quebecers have amply proved their staunch attachment to democratic principles, their attitude towards manifestations of otherness is fraught with the ambivalence typical of a nation whose own future is uncertain, whose minority status within a wider global socioeconomic context leaves it at the margins of history. Indeed they inevitably tend to oscillate between a laudable democratic impulse -- which calls for sociopolitical inclusiveness and the development of an enlarged citizenship -- and the fear of losing parts of their historically determined identity, of seeing their community fall into political irrelevance.[28] If allowed to express itself and

---

[28] Létourneau & Ruel, "Nous Autres les Québécois. Topiques du discours franco-québécois sur Soi et l'Autre dans les mémoires déposés devant la Commission Bélanger-Campeau," in Fall, Simeoni, & Vignaux (eds.), *Mots représentations: Enjeux dans les contacts interethniques et interculturels*, 283-307 (1994); Ruel, "Entre la rhétorique et la mémoire: usages du passé et références à l'histoire dans les mémoires déposés devant la Commission

dominate the political process, this fear would irremediably stifle the democratic inspiration of the *Parti Québécois*'s civic nationalism.

There are two possible responses to the challenge posed by NAFTA and globalization to Quebec's sovereignty and cultural integrity. The Quebec government could impose its steamrolling power to level off differences and various claims for the inclusion of distinctive identities in the public space. In this respect, it would not act any differently than most governments of liberal states. Liberal political and administrative cultures generally tend to celebrate in principle subjective and individual identities, on the one hand, but actually emphasize formal equality and identical treatment of individuals and communities, on the other. Liberal politics may theoretically encourage diversity and pluralism, but in the end it actualizes itself in the homogenizing fusion of differences into one overarching system of government. Given the current political dispositions, this is the path in which the Quebec government is most likely to engage naturally.

The other response, though improbable on the short run, is not implausible on the long run, given a proper mobilization of emerging heterogenic social forces in Quebec. Quebec society could engage in a process of identity redefinition based on cultural *métissage* and the development of an enlarged, thoroughly inclusionary sphere of citizenship. Such a process would undoubtedly be in line with the aspirations of those who strive for a "transcultural" Quebec. Globalization, in this sense, could be at the source of a new political community whose *raison d'être* and defining logic, however, would bear little resemblance to that which sovereignists are currently longing for. Their implicit understanding of the nation as a modern, autonomous, and sovereign form of political rationality is particularly questionable in the current context of heterogenic expressions.

For all that, Quebec nationalists and sovereignists have welcomed NAFTA and endorsed its underlying globalizing and modernist force. What they see as the virtues of that trade agreement may well, in the end, signal the beginning of a new era of post-sovereignty[29] where sovereignty would be, in fact, a meaningless objective. As Partha Chatterjee[30] has aptly noted: "Nationalism .

---

sur l'avenir politique et constitutionnel du Québec (1990)," 6 *Discours social/Social Discourse*, 213-242 (1994).

[29]   Breton, "De la mondialisation: ses contraintes, ses défis, ses enjeux," in Breton, Fecteau, & Létourneau (eds.), *La condition québécoise: Enjeux et horizons d'une société en devenir* 19-40 (1994).

[30]   P. Chatterjee, *Nationalist Thought and the Colonial World: A Derivative Discourse* (1986).

. . seeks to represent itself in the image of the Enlightenment and fails to do so. For Enlightenment itself, to assert its sovereignty as the universal ideal, needs its Other; if it could ever actualise itself in the real world as the truly universal, *it would in fact destroy itself.*"[31] This might well be a risk Quebec sovereignists will have to run.

---

[31] Quoted in Bhabha, "DissimiNation: Time, Narrative, and the Margins of the Modern Nation," in Bhabha (ed.), *Nation and Narration* 293 (1990) (emphasis added).

Chapter Five

CULTURAL IDENTITY IN THE UNITED STATES: WILL NAFTA CHANGE AMERICA?

by Jill Norgren and Serena Nanda

1. INTRODUCTION

The creation of a national identity in the United States occurred in the context of significant differences in ethnicity, race, religious persuasion, and social class. These differences produced conflict over the values that would govern the new American society. The availability of land permitted early settlers, and later, migrants from the East Coast, to avoid much of this conflict and to protect their differences by moving. Religious dissenters, led by Ann Hutchinson and Roger Williams, left the Massachusetts Bay to form the new colony of Rhode Island in 1664; the Mormons, fleeing persecution, trekked across the United States and beyond its borders to the Great Salt Lake Basin to find a haven for their unique culture in the 1840s; and in the period after World War II, no longer valuing the diversity of urban culture, and liberated by the automobile, America's growing middle class drove to the suburbs, where in relative isolation from surrounding cities, they created a suburban culture based on the values of homeowning, highways, and homogeneity.

Simultaneous with this development of local cultures, however, there has been the emergence of an "American" culture and identity. The people who first came here were Anglo-Saxon, Christian, and in spite of a few communal groups, predominantly adherents of eighteenth century liberal individualism. In coming here, they sought to fulfill a vision of a "new Eden" that, when married to the emerging concept of the nation state, encouraged the building of a common

D. G. Dallmeyer (ed.), Joining Together, Standing Apart: National Identities after NAFTA, 91–109.
© 1997 Kluwer Law International. Printed in the Netherlands.

national culture. The national identity that developed is expressed in dominant U.S. cultural values including democracy, capitalism, individualism, competition, the nuclear family, and patriarchy. This identity also is shaped by a history of racism and the tension between secularism, on the one hand, and a commitment to the spiritual traditions of the Old and New Testaments, on the other.

Through legislation and court decisions, the United States has long defended the dominant culture values that shape this American identity against challenges raised by subcultural groups. In this chapter we review decisions of state and national courts that reveal the limits of cultural pluralism in the United States. These examples support our judgment that the North American Free Trade Agreement (NAFTA) is unlikely to provide a substantial stimulus for changes in U.S. cultural identity. Based on these court decisions, we argue that the people of the United States evidence little interest in abandoning their "American" identity. To the contrary, Americans have held fiercely to a relatively fixed set of values over the course of their two hundred year history, marginalizing, and sometimes imprisoning, those who would not agree to live by dominant culture values. Thus, although the United States is correctly described as a multi-cultural society with many large and flourishing subcultures, in law certain cultural identities and norms are privileged over others. NAFTA is not likely to alter this reality even as the exchange of products and services across the borders of Mexico, Canada, and the United States increases and, in the process, expands our knowledge of one another. In the United States, the formation of "Little ... (Mexico, India, Korea)" communities will continue, so-called ethnic restaurants will abound, and foreign language radio and television will proliferate. Transnational cultures have and will continue to take shape in response to the ease of travel, the ubiquity of television, and the spread of phone, fax, and Internet-enhanced communication. NAFTA, however, will not change the commitment to America's dominant culture values. Moreover, contemporary political action, including English-only laws and California's Proposition 187, suggests a strong resistance to alteration of this dominant cultural political identity and, in some regions, an increase in ethnocentrism and racism.

2. LAW: A TOOL FOR MAINTAINING CULTURAL IDENTITY

The United States, with its liberal constitutional political system, has experienced a fundamental tension between the need to create national institutions, including law, that unify its culturally different groups and the need to safeguard human rights by permitting some amount of cultural and local political autonomy. The United States, as a nation under the rule of law, has employed legislation and court decisions as important mechanisms for addressing this tension between the need for national consensus around a dominant set of cultural values and institutions, and the demands of subcultural groups wishing to protect their autonomy or to be free of stigmatizing law.

Throughout the history of the United States, culturally different groups and local, state, and federal government have confronted each other in legislatures and in courts. They have joined battle when government has sought to marginalize, or frankly prohibit, cultural differences and they have met when government has sought to keep culturally different groups separate and disadvantaged. It is a legal history of getting in, and staying out.

The history of the struggle of subcultural groups to protect language rights in the United States is particularly germane to the evaluation of NAFTA's impact on American national identity. Litigation involving language rights provides a means to examine the limits of cultural tolerance in the United States and the likelihood of the legal sanctioning of linguistic pluralism.

The United States does not have an official national language. Local and national language policies have been inconsistent, reflecting territorial expansion, changing immigration patterns, and perceived threats to American national security. There was no consensus in our eighteenth century national constitutional debate over language and the Constitution itself does not define English, or any other language, as the official language of the country. At the state level, the language of European settlers was sometimes permitted or even encouraged within an implicit or explicit context of English as the official language. But some states also outlawed languages other than English. Expansion westward, annexation of Mexican territory, and later Hawaii and Puerto Rico, added other elements to United States language policy.

In the nineteenth century, Native Americans, viewed as a group that needed to overcome "tribal barbarism" and to assimilate, were forced to send their children to boarding schools, often hundreds of miles from local communities, so that they would be permanently wrenched from their cultures and languages. Strenuous efforts to convert immigrant and territorial populations to speaking English became a central mission of American public schools and helped to make compulsory education laws popular as they were introduced in the second half of the nineteenth century. Many Americans were in complete accord with the earlier statement of New York politician De Witt Clinton that, "The triumph and adoption of the English language have been the principal means of melting us down into one people, and of extinguishing those stubborn prejudices and violent animosities which formed a wall of partition between the inhabitants of the same land."[1]

Language affirms identity and provides an important boundary between people of one nation state and those of another. Benedict Andersen has written that the "imagined communities" that become nations are often identified primarily in terms of language.[2] Language has obvious and important functions as a medium of communication in economic, political, and social life. But language has important expressive meaning for subcultures within the nation. A shared language is a central vehicle for conveying individual and cultural identity and for expressing the intimacy of social relations within an ethnic group and community. Language, unlike ethnic costume, is not a relic in the United States for many ethnic groups. The ability to adapt language to new situations enables it to become part of the vitality of a subculture. Thus, while the United States has no official language, there have been legal confrontations over acceptance and public recognition of the second languages kept alive by American subcultures.

The legal controversies concerning language have occurred in the context of voting, court testimony, the conduct of government business, and education. The courtroom debates have reflected, on the one hand, the view that American citizens must share a common language in which to conduct common affairs, and, on the other, the belief that cultural diversity enriches society and cannot be suppressed by unconstitutional means.

Early in the twentieth century conflict over language policy emerged in our schools. World War I led to increased xenophobia; speaking and teaching a foreign language were identified with disloyalty to the United States. Laws were passed in many states prohibiting the teaching of languages other than English in public, or even private, schools. At that time, these laws fell particularly heavily on German immigrants, who were a large minority using, in many communities, private schools to preserve their language. When Nebraska convicted Robert Meyer of violating such a statute by teaching the Bible, in German, to elementary school children, he appealed to the United States Supreme Court. The Court's response in *Meyer v. Nebraska* [262 U.S. 390 (1923)] initiated an approach that has informed much subsequent legal reasoning in cultural identity litigation. In *Meyer*, the majority argued that:

> The salutary purpose of the statute is clear. The legislature had seen the baneful effects of permitting foreigners who had taken residence in this country, to rear and educate their children in the language of their native land. The result of that condition was found to be inimical to our own safety. To allow the children of foreigners ... to be

---

[1]   Steven Steinberg, *The Ethnic Myth* 9 (1981).
[2]   *See generally*, Benedict Anderson, *Imagined Communities* (1991).

taught from early childhood the language of the country of their parents, was to rear them with that language as their mother tongue. It was to educate them so that they must always think in that language, and, as a consequence, naturally inculcate in them the ideas and sentiments foreign to the best interests of this country.

The Court, however, concluded that the statute "as applied is arbitrary" and ruled in favor of *Meyer*. While acknowledging the desirability of the fostering of a homogeneous people through law, the justices asserted that "the individual has certain fundamental rights which must be respected." It violated constitutional due process to require that Meyer teach in English and, thus, deny, the values and traditions of his ethnic community. More than half a century later, opponents of the English-only movement draw on the procedural and substantive due process outlined in *Meyer*. At the same time, there can be no question that the Court's majority believed English to constitute a singularly important ingredient for America's melting pot.

It is necessary to observe, in the context of our discussion of NAFTA, that the impact of the ideology of English as the dominant language in the United States has been particularly burdensome for Latinos, who more than any other ethnic group have retained their language; indeed, the use of Spanish among Latinos is increasing, along with an increase in their acquisition of English. As a result of immigration, population growth, and language maintenance, Spanish is the most widely-used (non-English) language in the United States. But Anglos have largely viewed the persistence of Spanish language on the part of, for example, Mexican Americans, Puerto Ricans, and Cuban Americans, as an insuperable barrier to Latino-American patriotism, and to the incorporation of Latinos into mainstream legal, economic, social, and educational institutions in the United States. Much -- though not all -- public policy and court decisions reflect a reluctance to acknowledge or support the use of Spanish language and express a clear opposition toward the modification of Anglo-American culture to include elements of Latino culture.

Latinos in the United States are a diverse group and, collectively, one of the largest ethnic minority populations in the country. As of 1989, there were approximately 21 million Latino immigrants and their descendants in the United States, constituting just under 10 percent of the population. Of these, thirteen million were Mexican Americans. Mexican Americans originate in the populations of the Southwest and California, whose settlement predated the 1846-1848 Mexican American War. The United States defeated Mexico in that war, conquering a vast region composed of California, New Mexico, and parts of Colorado, Arizona, and Nevada. In the Treaty of Guadalupe Hidalgo ending the war, the United States guaranteed the property and religious rights of the approximately 80,000 inhabitants living in the newly acquired area.[3] The treaty notwithstanding, land rights were disregarded and the non-Anglo inhabitants were subjected to discrimination and harassment that varied by territory. In Colorado and Arizona, the Mexican community remained separate from the Anglo population but was tolerated; in Texas and California, early toleration subsequently changed to discrimination and repression.[4] Until the 1920s, Spanish and English were recognized as co-official languages in New Mexico, where all state documents were printed in Spanish. But the United States did not admit either New Mexico or Arizona to statehood until the Anglos had attained a majority and could assure the formal commitment of the state to the dominant culture values of the United States.

Contemporary language litigation involving Spanish-speaking communities has grown out of conflicts in schools, voting places, and courtrooms. Numerous recent appeals of criminal convictions, for example, have focused on the failure of the government to provide full translation of all proceedings. In other cases, defendants have objected to the use of preemptory challenges to excuse bilingual jurors who would not have to rely on the court-appointed translator.

Equally important court decisions involving Mexican Americans have addressed the role of language in the workplace. In the 1980 case of *Garcia v. Gloor* [618 F.2d 264], a federal court determined that an employer might impose a "speak-only-English" rule on his employees without violating provisions of the Equal Employment Act and the Civil Rights Act, 42 U.S.C. sections 1981 and 1985(c). The court concluded that the rule, in the case of twenty-four-year-old Hector Garcia, was not a burdensome condition of employment and did not produce an atmosphere of ethnic oppression.

Almost immediately the United States Equal Employment Opportunity Commission (EEOC), the federal agency charged with administering employment discrimination law, established guidelines that were contrary to the position of the court in *Garcia*. These rules held that a total prohibition on speaking languages other than English would be presumed invalid, and that a limited prohibition on speaking languages other than English would be permitted only when justified by a clear "business necessity," defined to include communications during emergencies and while conducting inherently dangerous work. Courts in the mid-1980s appeared to be guided by the EEOC's openness to the expression

---

[3]   O'Brien, "Cultural Rights in the United States: A Conflict of Values," 5 *Law & Inequality* 267, 329-30 (1987). These guarantees are contained in, Treaty of Guadalupe Hidalgo, T.S. No. 207, 9 Stat. 922 (Arts. VII and IX).

[4]   O'Brien, *supra* note 3, at 330. We draw on O'Brien for this history.

of cultural identity in the workplace. In 1993, however, the Ninth Circuit Court of Appeals in California took issue with the EEOC guidelines. In *Garcia v. Spun Steak Company* [998 F.2d 1480], a challenge to a workplace English-only rule, the appeals court held that, "Title VII does not protect the ability of workers to express their cultural heritage at the workplace; it is concerned only with dispar-ities in treatment of workers and does not confer substantive privileges. ... It is axiomatic that an employee often must sacrifice individual self-expression during working hours ... there is nothing in Title VII which requires an employer to allow employees to express their cultural identity." Despite this conflict between the opinion of an important appeals court and the EEOC, and with over 100 workplace English-only cases pending at the EEOC, the U.S. Supreme Court declined to hear an appeal of *Garcia v. Spun Steak*.

Language rights cases, although decided in the relatively restricted context of school, the courtroom, and the workplace, nevertheless address the more funda-mental issue of the willingness of American institutions to accept or encourage cultural diversity. The sentiment in many American courts, mirroring the domi-nant culture, is that cultural identity as expressed in the right to use a language other than English, is subordinate to the needs of the nation state for unity, and that "the social contract attenuates as it crosses linguistic ... lines."[5] It is also the case, however, that some courts and legislatures have acknowledged subcultural language rights in ordering the printing of bilingual ballots and the creation of bilingual school programs (but as "tools of transition" to speaking English). The increasing number of non-English-speaking immigrants, and bilin-gual Americans, undoubtedly will provoke further national debate in the United States on the question of language rights. The failure of the Supreme Court to participate in *Garcia v. Spun Steak* will not decrease the pressure for English-only rules, as there is an unflinching belief in many communities that our nation-al identity, and our national success, are tied to one language: English. If a future North American trade or economic union agreement should open the bor-ders of the United States to people, in addition to goods and services, the lan-guage debate, with its fundamental connection to cultural and political identity, will only intensify.

We began this essay by asserting that NAFTA would not have a substantial effect on the national or cultural identity of the United States. We argued that the people of the United States have held fiercely to a fixed set of values including the dominance of English in public discourse. These values extend well beyond language into other facets of culture such as religious practices, race, and

---

5   *Guadalupe v. Tempe*, 578 F.2d 1022, 1027 (1978).

ethnicity. In order to support our contention, we now turn to judicial review of some of these facets of cultural identity: cases involving treatment of Native Americans, African Americans, Asians, and specific religious groups.

The early economic integration of Native American and colonial economies did not lead to cultural integration. Rather, from their first contacts, immigrants from England, France, and Spain rejected the creation of a cultural identity built on a mixing of Native American and Anglo-European cultures. Indeed, six-teenth-century Spaniards questioned whether Native Americans were humans in the sense of having the capacity to reason and to have a soul; eighteenth-century Americans determined that Native Americans were fools because they did not believe man had dominion over the land and all of its resources. The taking of Native American land was justified in the 1790s, but also in 1979, because they were viewed as incapable of "prudent management of their communal prop-erty."[6]

Law became an important tool used by the United States in the maintenance of cultural identity untouched by Native American values and practices. The U.S. Constitution reflects no knowledge or appreciation of Native American values although, at the time of its writing, colonists and Native Americans had lived side by side for nearly two hundred years and Native Americans had offered much help to the colonists. Subsequent American legislation and court decisions affirmed Anglo-American values and lifestyles while they stigmatized those of the Native American. For example, in a sequence of U.S. Supreme Court opinions directly or indirectly involving Native American land [*Fletcher v. Peck*, 10 U.S. 87 (1810); *Johnson v. M'Intosh*, 21 U.S. 543 (1823); *Cherokee Nation v. Georgia*, 30 U.S. 1 (1831); and *Worcester v. Georgia*, 31 U.S. 515 (1832)], Chief Justice John Marshall built the foundation of an American law of continental real estate by which the United States could claim a legal rather than an outlaw's title to the land. Marshall drew upon Anglo-American ideas of private property and ignored the communal norms that governed most Native American assignment of land.

Resistance to the integration of Anglo-American identity with that of Native American societies was further expressed in U.S. removal policy articulated in the 1830 Removal Act. For decades the law of removal, by which the United States forced the permanent resettlement of entire Native American communities to the western side of the Mississippi River, dominated American policy. In this period, but particularly in the second half of the nineteenth century, the United States also pursued an aggressive politics of Native American assimilation. Pop-

---

[6]   Brief for Petitioner at 48, *United States v. Sioux*, 448 U.S. 371 (1980) (No. 79-639).

ular knowledge today focuses upon the Indian boarding schools where non-Indian teachers sought to divorce Indian children from all knowledge of, and respect for, their own cultures and identities. Less well known is the 1887 Dawes General Allotment Act, legislation by which the government of the United States sought, using the legal principle of fee simple title, to end the communal landbase and cultures of Native American nations near its borders.

Grounded in the spirit of economic destiny and superiority, the United States capped this history of cultural misanthropy by declaring, in 1903, a sweeping trust power over "our Indian ward." The relationship of the United States to Native Americans in the twentieth century was guided by this declaration of paternalistic prerogative. Only over the past thirty years has the United States turned its back on the worst of this turn-of-the-century legal doctrine. Yet, even as the federal government re-examines the law that has disenfranchised and disadvantaged Native Americans, the idea of integrating organizing principles of Native American culture -- communalism, consensus-building, and a shared landbase -- remains alien to virtually all Americans.

The experience of Africans brought forcibly to North America, as well as that of Asian immigrants, was little different from that of the indigenous Native American population. Each of these groups was marginalized by an Anglo-American citizenry that evidenced little interest in -- indeed, antipathy to -- the blending of cultural identities. For example, in the 1880s when the federal government committed itself to the destruction of Native American cultures, Congress also passed the Chinese Exclusion Act (1882). This legislation barred all Chinese laborers from entering the country for ten years (this was extended later) in an effort to limit economic competition from Chinese workers and to insulate American society already living in the United States and required that they carry identity papers, a decree specific to them. A decade later, in 1896, the U.S. Supreme Court sanctioned the practice of legal segregation of Americans by race in its infamous decision, *Plessy v. Ferguson* [163 U.S. 537].

The limits of cultural pluralism and American resistance to the integration of Anglo-American culture by that of new immigrants from non-Western nations also was expressed in the internment of Japanese Americans during World War II. Like the Chinese, Japanese immigration had been severely restricted by the U.S. government in the first half of the twentieth century on the grounds that they were willing to assimilate and that they were willing to work for low wages. Following the attack on Pearl Harbor, Japanese Americans as a group were accused of being clannish and a security threat. Americans who made these accusations ignored the existence of local and state laws that isolated Japanese American and Japanese immigrant communities and encouraged them to aid one another -- laws prohibiting Japanese from owning land, for example, or leasing it for more than three years, as well as *de jure* school segregation, and laws prohibiting Asians from marrying Caucasians.

The determination of the United States that Japanese Americans (but not German Americans) and resident Japanese aliens posed a threat to the security of the United States led to upwards of 120,000 members of these two groups first being put under curfew and then forcibly evacuated to detention camps. Because of their group identity, most spent three years behind barbed wire, denied individual loyalty-security hearings until a Supreme Court decision in 1944 [*Ex Parte Endo*, 323 U.S. 284]. But it is important to understand the extent to which they were the victims of cultural fears and economic greed as well as military concerns. Japanese Americans were viewed as being unacceptably different; many also farmed newly irrigated lands in California desired by Caucasian farmers. After Pearl Harbor white farm business organizations sent lobbyists to Washington who manipulated the national security hysteria in their interests. The speech of Austin Anson, managing secretary of the Salinas Vegetable Grower-Shipper Association, was not atypical of the openly expressed racism endured by Japanese Americans:

> We are charged with wanting to get rid of the Japs for selfish reasons. ... We do. It's a question of whether the white man lives on the Pacific Coast or the brown men. They came into this valley to work, and they stayed to take over. ... They undersell the white man in the markets ... they work their women and children while the white farmer has to pay wages for his help. If all the Japs were removed tomorrow, we'd never miss them in two weeks, because the white farmer can take over and produce everything the Jap does. And we don't want them back when the war ends, either.[7]

Japanese Americans and resident alien Japanese challenged the curfew and evacuation regulations imposed by the U.S. military (under President Roosevelt's authorization) before the U.S. Supreme Court. The Court upheld the orders in *Hirabayashi v. United States* [320 U.S. 81 (1943)] and *Korematsu v. United States* [323 U.S. 214 (1944)], arguing "hardships are a part of war, and war is an aggregation of hardships." Justice Frank Murphy argued otherwise, however, forcefully characterizing the government's policy as one motivated by racism and ethnocentrism, rather than military necessity:

> ... the result in good measure of this erroneous assumption of racial guilt rather than bona fide military necessity is evidenced by the Commanding General's Final Report on the evacuation from the Pacific Coast area. In it he refers to all individuals of Japanese descent as "subversive," as belonging to "an enemy race" whose "racial

---

[7] *Korematsu v. United States*, 323 U.S. 214, 239 (1944).

strains are undiluted," and as constituting "over 112,000 potential enemies ... at large today" along the Pacific Coast. In support of this blanket condemnation of all persons of Japanese descent, however, no reliable evidence is cited to show that such individuals were generally disloyal. ... Individuals of Japanese ancestry are condemned because they are said to be "a large, unassimilated, tightly knit racial group, bound to an enemy nation by strong ties of race, culture, custom and religion." [This is] cited as evidence of possible group disloyalty. ... The main reasons relied upon by those responsible for the forced evacuation, therefore, do not prove a reasonable relation between the group characteristics of Japanese Americans and the dangers of invasion, sabotage, and espionage. The reasons appear, instead to be largely an accumulation of much of the misinformation, half-truths and insinuations that for years have been directed against Japanese Americans by people with racial and economic prejudices -- the same people who have been among the foremost advocates of the evacuation. A military judgment based upon such racial and sociological considerations is not entitled to the great weight ordinarily given the judgments based upon strictly military considerations ... [T]o infer that examples of individual disloyalty prove group disloyalty and justify discriminatory action against the entire group is to deny that under our system of law individual guilt is the sole basis for deprivation of rights. Moreover, this inference, which is at the very heart of the evacuation orders, has been used in support of the abhorrent and despicable treatment of minority groups by the dictatorial tyrannies which this nation is now pledged to destroy. To give constitutional sanction to that inference in this case, however well intentioned may have been the military command on the Pacific Coast, is to adopt one of the cruelest of the rationales used by our enemies to destroy the dignity of the individual and to encourage and open the door to discriminatory actions against other minority groups in the passions of tomorrow.

I dissent, therefore, from this legalization of racism.[8]

Forty-five years later the United States government, following the passage in Congress of the "Civil Liberties Act," offered a formal apology to the victims of its wartime policies of internment, characterizing them as a grave injustice to Japanese Americans. A reparations program was put in place under the authority of the Office of Redress Administration. As of December 1994, 79,515 individuals have qualified for the US$20,000 payment.

Language, race, and ethnicity have not been the sole challenges to the American myth of the melting pot. As members of the Church of Latter-Day Saints, often called Mormons, have discovered, there are decided legal limits to American tolerance of religious pluralism.

Mormonism originated in the 1820s religious experience of a young New York man named Joseph Smith. The church he founded was almost immediately attacked by other Christians because of the extravagant nature of his religious

---

[8]   *Korematsu v. United States*, 323 U.S. 214 (1944). Murphy dissented in this case. In preliminary voting in *Hirabayashi*, Murphy indicated that he would dissent. Under strong pressure from Justice Felix Frankfurter, he agreed to change his vote and to side with the majority. His concurring opinion, however, barely veiled his distaste for the Court's holding.

claims of seeing God and angels, and his interpretation of scriptures. The Mormons moved west to avoid persecution, eventually settling in the Great Salt Lake Basin. They established a theocratic state with a communitarian economy. Some members of the community practiced polygyny (men having more than one wife). Shortly thereafter the basin area in which they lived became U.S. territory following war with Mexico. Although in many ways the lives of the Saints (as they called themselves) resembled those of other western pioneers, Mormons were identified as having rejected important tenets of American culture: the secular political state; a capitalist economy; and the nuclear family and monogamy.

Popular outrage against the Mormons grew. In 1856 leaders of the new Republican Party declared that polygamy in Utah Territory should be equated with Southern slavery as the "twin relics of barbarism." American officials regarded polygamists as criminals. In 1857, President Buchanan sent 5,000 troops to occupy the Salt Lake Valley in order to serve notice to the Mormons that flouting the law of the United States would not be allowed. The occupation failed.

Unable to alter the beliefs and practices of church members in this fashion, federal and territorial governments turned to the further use of law. From 1862, when Congress passed the Morrill Antibigamy Act, until 1890 when the leadership of the Church of Latter-Day Saints renounced polygyny, the U.S. government carried out an aggressive legal campaign intent upon undermining the power of the Mormon Church and ending the economic communalism, theocracy, and polygamy practiced by its members.

The assault on the Church of Latter-Day Saints challenged the idea that the United States had no particular religious orthodoxy. Certainly the Mormons believed that the Constitution's First Amendment religious guarantees did not establish an official religion, and that the Establishment and Free Exercise Clauses insured the toleration of religious differences. But the religious rights they asserted before the United States Supreme Court were strongly rejected in three seminal late-nineteenth century cases: *Reynolds v. United States* [98 U.S. 146 (1879)]; *Davis v. Beason* [133 U.S. 333 (1889)]; and *Romney v. United States* [136 U.S. 1 (1889)]. In *Reynolds* the Court upheld federal antibigamy legislation, asserting the sanctity of monogamy and its central place in American culture. Legally, the Court based its decision upon a new belief/action doctrine. According to the Court, the First Amendment guaranteed the right to hold any religious opinion but not necessarily the right to act according to that belief. In fact, the Court's decision rested upon deeply held cultural assumptions, laced with an anti-Asian bias, clearly stated in the majority opinion written by Chief Justice Morrison Waite:

Polygamy has always been odious among the northern and western nations of Europe, and, until the establishment of the Mormon Church, was almost exclusively a feature of the life of Asiatic and of African people. At common law, the second marriage was always void and from the earliest history of England polygamy has been treated as an offence against society ... it is impossible to believe that the constitutional guaranty of religious freedom was intended to prohibit legislation in respect to this most important feature of social life. Marriage, while from its very nature a sacred obligation, is nevertheless, in most civilized nations, a civil contract, and usually regulated by law. Upon it society may be said to be built, and out of its fruits spring social relations and social obligations and duties, with which government is necessarily required to deal. In fact, according as monogamous or polygamous marriages are allowed, do we find the principles on which the government of the people, to a greater or lesser extent, rests ... polygamy leads to the patriarchal principle, and which, when applied to large communities, fetters the people in stationary despotism, while that principle cannot long exist in connection with monogamy. ... Laws are made for the government of actions, and while they cannot interfere with mere religious belief and opinions, they may with practices. Suppose one believed that human sacrifices were a necessary part of religious worship, would it be seriously contended that the civil government under which he lived could not interfere to prevent a sacrifice? Or if a wife religiously believed it was her duty to burn herself upon the funeral pyre of her dead husband, would it be beyond the power of the civil government to prevent her carrying her belief into practice? ...

The conclusion that there were, in the Court's words, "enlightened sentiments of mankind" to which all religious groups must conform, informed the next two Mormon cases, *Davis* and Romney. In *Davis* Justice Stephen Field argued that, "Bigamy and polygamy are crimes by the laws of all civilized and Christian countries." His opinion focused upon the moral threat posed by the lifestyle of the Mormons and claimed an important connection between the monogamous family and "free, self-governing commonwealth[s]."

The implacable hostility of the United States and its adamant refusal to accommodate Mormon communalism, theocracy, and its "peculiar" custom of polygamy led church leaders to concede that in order to survive confiscation of its property and to gain statehood it would have to renounce polygamy, dissolve the church party, and refashion aspects of its economy. In October 1890, following the announcement of an instructive revelation received by Mormon leader Wilford Woodruff, the Church formally repudiated the practice of polygyny.

While the overwhelming membership of the Church of Latter-Day Saints has now adapted to a set of values in considerable opposition to its original theology, and even as Mormons are portrayed as a model of capitalistic enterprise and moral respectability, there are twentieth-century Mormons who have refused to make any accommodation to the dominant culture. These "fundamentalists" are excommunicated by their church and continue to provoke legal confrontation with government authorities. These Mormons defend polygyny as a "straighter line to God" and polygyny remains at the center of their understanding of religious doctrine, identity, and community. There are as many as 30,000 to 50,000 men, women, and children living in such polygamous households in the United States. While the last major government raid on a polygamous community occurred in the 1950s, adherence to polygyny has more recently provoked legal dispute over, for example, the right to adopt.

The legal experience of the Amish when seeking to exempt their children from compulsory educational laws, stands in marked contrast to that of the Mormons and suggests that the legal treatment of the Mormons was an aberration. Yet, this is not the case. The Amish, the Native American Church, and other religious groups whose practices have been challenged but ultimately sanctioned in American law share characteristics that permitted American courts and Americans themselves to treat them differently from the Mormons.

The Amish, a pious Anabaptist Christian people, appear strikingly different in dress, practices, and language from the surrounding twentieth-century American world. The central value in Amish life is submission to a higher authority, which entails resignation of God's will, yielding to others, self-denial, contentment, and quiet spirit. The religion of the Amish life is woven into the fabric of everyday life: religion, culture, and community are inseparable. Amish life is guided by Christian principles, emphasizes the connection to local community, and rejects most aspects of modernity and materialism. These principles of living, enunciated by church leaders in the seventeenth century, put Amish in conflict with the secular, bureaucratized, technologically complex, individualistic, rights-oriented culture of twentieth-century America.

It is not surprising that a major conflict between the Amish and local government authorities arose over the question of sending Amish children to non-Amish public high schools. Schools are an important agent of socialization into the ideas and practices of the dominant culture. In the post-World War II era, the Amish sought to promote their children being "in the world but not of it" by prohibiting them from attending the large, consolidated high schools that had become increasingly common in the rural farm areas. Cited for violating state compulsory education laws, Amish parents declared that their actions were protected by the constitutional guarantee of free exercise of religion.

The U.S. Supreme Court agreed that, in this case, Amish religious rights outweighed the state's interest in universal education (the Amish asked that their children be exempt from compulsory schooling from age 14 to 16). The opinion of the Court in *Wisconsin v. Yoder* [406 U.S. 205 (1973)] reflects profoundly upon the question of cultural identities in America. The reasoning employed in the opinion was guided by three understandings: first, that the Amish were not aggressive proselytizers seeking to convert other Americans to their unique lifestyle; second, the Amish were a self-sufficient, law-abiding, productive, and morally righteous community; and, third, the Amish, while evoking another age in their dress and their rejection of modernity, taught their children English, lived in nuclear families, and accepted the principles of the market economy. In spite of the desire of the Amish to separate from the world, the justices viewed theirs as a model community, an idealized picture of rural, hard-working America which, while fast disappearing, played an important role in our identity and history. Amish beliefs and practices, while in many ways distinctly different from mainstream twentieth-century American culture, were not understood by the Court to threaten the dominant culture.

This is the key to understanding many of the religious freedom cases. The belief and practices of the Church of Latter-Day Saints challenged several of the fundamental values of American society. The Mormons were as self-sufficient as the Amish, but because Mormon self-sufficiency was communal and socialistic, allied with the repugnant practice of polygyny, and supported by theocratic politics, American courts -- speaking for the dominant culture -- determined to repress the Mormons.

A comparison of two churches that espouse the religious use of drugs as a path to religious insight similarly demonstrates the willingness of the dominant culture, as represented by its courts, to tolerate difference only when it can be understood within dominant culture values. This is illustrated by the recent legal experience of the Native American Church and the Ethiopian Zion Coptic Church. When the State of California prosecuted members of the Native American Church for the religious use of the proscribed substance, peyote, the California State Supreme Court struck down the conviction arguing, in part, that the Church incorporated familiar elements of Christianity. The court in this case, *People v. Woody* [61 Cal. 2d 716 (1964)], presented the Native American Church as a small, quietistic Christian subculture whose members had no political or social agenda perceived as threatening to the dominant American culture. Unlike the Native American Ghost Dance of the late nineteenth century, and other Native American revitalization movements, Native American church peyotism does not emphasize a change in the social order. It is not informed, for example, by a vision of whites disappearing and the land once again in the possession of Native American nations.

In contrast, the conviction of members of the Ethiopian Zion Coptic Church, also known as Rastafarians, for the religious use of marijuana, has been upheld in most American courts. The theology of the Ethiopian Zion Coptic Church blends elements of Christianity with an African consciousness. Despite the connection to Christianity, however, judges have adopted a largely hostile posture toward Rastafarian drug use, not finding it protected by the Free Exercise Clause. The public unwillingness to grant a religious exemption for the use of marijuana comparable to that authorized for peyote arises from the perception that the Rastafarians are an alien and threatening subculture. In contrast with the Native American Church, Rastafarians make frequent and open use of marijuana and are willing to sell it. Some congregations permit children to use it as a sacrament. Rastafarian dress and hairstyle distance them from a majority of the American population, even more than Native American Church members. The general perception of Rastafarianism as an "imported" religion further increases the difficulty of their acceptance as does their association with the condemnation of wage labor. Thus, while the central legal issue for each church has been the claim of religious exemption from laws proscribing drug use, their treatment in American courts has turned, in large measure, upon the degree to which each was seen as being in opposition to the dominant American society.

3. CONCLUSION

American courts have responded inconsistently to the claims of culturally diverse groups. Judges have reasoned that, "the freedom to differ is not limited to things that do not matter much ... the test of its substance is the right to differ as to things that touch the heart of the existing order."[9] But jurists also have limited the rights granted subcultural groups by arguing that, "cultural diversity within the nation-state, whatever may be its advantages from time to time, can restrict the scope of the fundamental compact. Diversity limits unity. ..."[10]

These contrasting statements by two federal court justices illustrate the polar views that American law has adopted with respect to cultural diversity. Despite the stark polarity of their viewpoints, however, the legal process by which the rights of cultural minorities are considered appears to be guided by the existence and interaction of a number of predictable factors. One of the most important of these factors is the distance of the cultural activity that the group seeks to protect or promote, from the values of the dominant culture -- that is, democracy, individualism, capitalism, patriarchy and the nuclear family, religious ideas grounded in the Old and New Testaments, and the importance of the English language. Where American courts have accommodated distinct cultural identities which challenge or contradict "American" values, they have done so, as in the

---

[9]　*West Virginia v. Barnette*, 319 U.S. 624, 642 (1943).
[10]　*Guadalupe v. Tempe Elementary School District*, 587 F.2d 1022, 1027 (1978).

Native American Church peyote case and with the Amish, by describing the most narrow, culturally specific parameters within which the group's behavior would be sanctioned.

It would be a mistake to view the values of the dominant culture, as expressed in judicial decisions and opinions, as unchanging. A second factor that helps to explain the decisions in cultural identity cases is the application of evolving standards over time. This is most clear in the example of women and African Americans. In nineteenth-century America the Supreme Court could and did present African Americans as property to be used and moved at the will of their owners. Similarly in the nineteenth century, justices repeatedly based legal decisions affecting women's rights on stereotypes of women as timid, delicate, incapable of reasoning, and "unfit for many of the occupations of civil life."[11] As we move toward the end of the twentieth century, these cultural visions of African Americans and women no longer are expressed in legal decisions.

In another way, also, history explains the legal treatment of culturally different groups. In particular, in periods of national insecurity such as wartime, culturally different groups whose behaviors appear threatening to national interests find their rights only reluctantly affirmed, as in the Jehovah's Witnesses' challenge of a mandatory flag salute, or even trampled on, as with the Japanese Americans. The treatment of the Mormons, too, can be explained by national security interests -- the need of the then young nation of the United States to affirm and extend its hegemony. (This may explain why fundamentalist Mormons largely have been ignored by local and national government in the second half of the twentieth century).

Where national security is not at issue, and where the size and strength of the group pose no discernible challenge to the political, economic, and social order, court decisions favoring group rights are more likely. The Supreme Court's support for Amish parents wishing to withdraw their children from the final two years of compulsory education rests explicitly on the Court's view that the Amish are not a threat to the social order but, to the contrary, a model of virtue. In contrast, judicial resistance to the assertion of language rights by Spanish-speaking Americans and resident aliens reflects, in part, a concern for the potential impact of this large community on the economic, political, and social life of the United States. The explicit threat that some judges perceive in these language cases is buttressed by the negative stereotypes applied to Latino communities (as in the campaign on behalf of Proposition 187 in California).

A number of court decisions in cases involving subcultural autonomy suggest

---

[11] *Bradwell v. Illinois*, 83 U.S. 130, 141 (1872).

that another principle, that of the "slippery slope," also affects outcomes. This concern over the force of precedent and the possibility of a domino-like effect has inhibited American courts from deciding in favor of large claims for economic redress, particularly the return of land demanded by Native Americans who have demonstrated the violation of lawful treaties by the United States. Language rights for Spanish-speaking communities, situated in judicial awareness of the growing size of these communities, similarly raises the specter of a slippery slope in the form of an unending series of claims.

This list of factors implies that courts are not autonomous, isolated bodies composed of justices neutral toward dominant culture norms and immune to contemporary politics. On the one hand, judges are sworn to uphold the law which commits them to constitutional rights and liberties; on the other hand, justices do not and cannot entirely free themselves from the dominant cultural context of which their courts are a part. Thus, subcultural groups, as they use courts, must be keenly aware that they are contesting the dominant culture in an institution of that same culture which, while committed to the autonomy of law, rights, and liberties, is also an instrument of a nation state committed to maintaining the unity of the larger body politic and its cultural identity.

We return then to the question of cultural integration following NAFTA with several concluding observations. First, the United States has limited its commitment to cultural integration from the earliest moments of its colonial history. This was true of its relationship with Native American societies, and it was further reflected in the highly restrictive immigration policies of the late nineteenth and early twentieth centuries -- policies aimed, in particular, at the exclusion of peoples who were neither European nor Caucasian. Second, the exclusion of non-Europeans, whether through Indian removal acts or restrictive immigration, facilitated the establishment of a dominant culture based on a limited set of ideas and practices. Further, government in the United States has responded to significant challenges to the values of this dominant culture through legislation, court action, and in the case of labor, race, and foreign policies, with physical force.

Taken together, this national history portrays a society strongly committed to the maintenance of a fixed identity that is permitted to change, at best, slowly and which, historically, has accepted newcomers and new ideas on its own terms. The United States signed NAFTA shaped by this history, clearly rejecting any of the forms of supranationalism or "pooled sovereignty" espoused, for example, by some advocates of European Community. We reiterate our earlier assertion that NAFTA is unlikely to provide a substantial stimulus for changes in national identity, particularly in light of the asymmetrical power relations among the three signatories. It is our view that the people of the United States do not believe that the need for expanding economic markets compels accommodation. Yet the presence and the growing numbers of newcomers in the United States who may not share the values of America's dominant culture suggest both that regional cultures will grow and that, without question, there will be further contest over the shaping of national identity in the United States.

Chapter Six

GOVERNMENT BY TRADE AGREEMENT

by David A. Wirth[*]

1. INTRODUCTION

During the debate over the North American Free Trade Agreement (NAFTA),[1] George Will published a column in which he criticized environmental elitists and others who would impede the "exhilaratingly unknowable future",[2] catalyzed by that compact. Mr. Will notwithstanding, some of the less desirable aspects of the agreement were anything but "unknowable," and indeed quite predictable, at the time of the negotiation and the subsequent domestic implementation of the pact. Moreover, particularly with the benefit of hindsight, certain aspects of the agreement are plainly anything but "exhilarating," especially from an environmental point of view.

The purpose of this chapter is, first, to identify and analyze some of the undesirable distortions in governmental processes resulting from NAFTA's negotiation and domestic implementation -- an effect that might be described as "government by trade agreement." Second, the chapter suggests reforms that might mitigate or eliminate some of the more objectionable of these aspects without doing a disservice to the underlying goals and purposes of international trade

[*] This work was supported by grants from the Creswell Foundation and the Frances Lewis Law Center of Washington and Lee University. Portions of this paper are based on the author's previously published work.
[1] North American Free Trade Agreement, Dec. 8, 11, 14 & 17, U.S.-Can.-Mex., *reprinted in* 32 *I.L.M.* 296, 612 (1993).
[2] Will, "Judicial Exhibitionism," Wash. Post, July 8, 1993, at A17.

D. G. Dallmeyer (ed.), Joining Together, Standing Apart: National Identities after NAFTA, 111–129.

agreements and that, indeed, might enhance their efficacy and legitimacy. In particular, the chapter identifies the following ways in which international trade agreements such as NAFTA, at least as currently structured, distort our national governmental processes:

- by constraining governmental regulatory authority;
- by subordinating multilateral environmental agreements to the international trade regime;
- by significantly reducing the opportunities for public participation in domestic lawmaking through the "fast track" process;
- by precluding public access to dispute settlement panels constituted under international trade agreements;
- by disrupting domestic federalism and federal-state relations; and
- by adversely affecting the administrative process in matters of domestic jurisdiction that fall within the scope of an international trade agreement.

2. ENVIRONMENTAL REGULATIONS AS BARRIERS TO TRADE

International trade agreements, at least to the extent that they govern national regulatory measures in the areas of environment and public health, contain primarily "negative" obligations. That is to say, international trade agreements do not generally contain affirmative requirements directing national governments to achieve certain minimum criteria in these areas. Rather, most obligations in trade agreements establish constraints on governmental actions -- the establishment of tariffs, quotas, standards that discriminate between imported and domestically manufactured goods, and the like. In other words, in international trade agreements governments generally promise to refrain from taking certain actions, as opposed to obligating themselves to undertake any affirmative steps. This approach arises from a view of liberalized trade as a situation of less, rather than greater, intervention by national governments in an international market in which, but for impediments in the form of national measures, goods would circulate freely.

So, for instance, both NAFTA and the GATT Uruguay Round[3] articulate so-called "trade disciplines" designed to prevent the adoption of arbitrary or exces-

---

[3]   Final Act Embodying the Results of the Uruguay Round of Multilateral Trade Negotiations, 33 *I.L.M.* 9 (1994).

sive limitations on pesticides in food that could interfere with trade.[4] The trade disciplines contained in recent international trade agreements are intended to circumscribe the regulatory authority of national governments so as to limit the abuse of putative environmental or public health claims for protectionist purposes, and not to establish minimum benchmarks for protection of the environment and public health. To that extent, these international trade agreements can be considered deregulatory instruments.

By contrast, environmental protection anticipates affirmative, governmentally-established requirements. Domestic and international environmental policies depend almost totally on governmental intervention in the marketplace to remedy market failures and to offset externalities. The trade and environment debate in large measure is a confrontation between these two central driving forces, both of which are intended to improve human welfare: one, environment, by encouraging greater governmental regulation; and the other, liberalized trade, by pressing toward less. If the balance is struck incorrectly, there is an obvious potential for trade agreements unduly to constrain domestic and international regulation to protect the environment and public health.

One of the principal flash points in the trade and environment debate has been the potential for environmental measures to act as non-tariff barriers to trade; that is, the abuse of environmental or public health regulations to achieve trade-related goals, such as preventing competition from foreign goods for protectionist purposes. The paradigm for the non-tariff barrier problem has been a ban imposed by the European Union (EU) on the use of growth hormones in beef, including imported meat. The United States, where these chemicals are permitted, has strongly objected to the ban as a non-tariff barrier to trade because that measure supposedly is not supported by scientific evidence.[5] Attention from the trade point of view to environmental and public health measures as potential non-tariff barriers to trade has sparked a reciprocal concern from the environmental side about the possibility that the net could be cast too widely, potentially exposing legitimate environmental, health and safety measures to attack from a trade perspective.

---

[4] *See generally* Wirth, "The Role of Science in the Uruguay Round and NAFTA Trade Disciplines," 27 *Cornell Int'l L.J.* 818 (1994).

[5] *See generally* Rothberg, Note, "From Beer to BST: Circumventing the GATT Standards Code's Prohibition on Unnecessary Obstacles to Trade," 75 *Minn. L. Rev.* 505 (1990); Froman, "Recent Developments, The United States-European Community Hormone Treated Beef Conflict," 30 *Harv. Int'l L.J.* 549 (1989); Halpern, "The U.S.-EC Hormone Beef Controversy and the Standards Code: Implications for the Application of Health Regulations to Agricultural Trade," 14 *N.C. J. Int'l L. & Com. Reg.* 135 (1989).

As it stands now, from the point of view of environmental and public health regulation, such as measures to protect the integrity of the food supply, the international trade regime is pretty much a no-win proposition. Consistent with the "negative" character of the obligations in international trade agreements, there are no mechanisms in NAFTA for assuring the implementation of minimum governmental measures. Moreover, once those policies that do exist are subjected to trade-based scrutiny, nothing more than maintenance of the status quo can be expected to result even in the best possible case. The NAFTA disciplines must also be read against the background of a persistent tightening of trade-based constraints in this area under the 1947 GATT. Only one of the environmental, conservation, and public health measures examined by a GATT dispute settlement panel whose validity turned on the availability of the article XX exceptions in that instrument has withstood such scrutiny.[6] Moreover, there is little or no evidence that any of the NAFTA countries have abused regulatory measures designed to protect human health -- the area of greatest concern from the point of view of attenuation of domestic regulatory authority -- as opposed to that of animals or plants.

Fortunately, this conflict between the "negative" obligations in trade agreements and the affirmative governmental action required to assure environmental quality is not inevitable or irreconcilable. Trade agreements could very well articulate minimum environmental standards. In fact, there is even a theoretical underpinning for this approach that is entirely consistent with the underlying goals of these trade agreements.

The failure to meet minimum environmental standards can be characterized from a trade point of view as an export subsidy that should be prohibited by, and actionable under, a trade regime. As it stands now, a nation's environmental policy is part of its inherent comparative advantage in international trade. The international trade regime creates incentives for exporting nations to relax their environmental policies to lower the prices of their exported goods and consequently to improve their international competitiveness. While some might feel otherwise, it is at least arguable that lax environmental policies ought not be

---

[6]   United States -- Taxes on Automobiles, *reprinted in* 33 *I.L.M.* 1399 (1994). *But cf.* United States -- Restrictions on Imports of Tuna, *reprinted in* 33 *I.L.M.* 842 (1994); United States -- Restrictions on Imports of Tuna, *Basic Instruments and Selected Documents*, 39th Supp. at 155 (1993), *reprinted in* 30 *I.L.M.* 1594 (1991); Thailand -- Restrictions on Importation of and Internal Taxes on Cigarettes, *Basic Instruments and Selected Documents*, 37th Supp. at 200 (1991), *reprinted in* 30 *I.L.M.* 1122 (1991); Canada -- Measures Affecting Exports of Unprocessed Herring and Salmon, *Basic Instruments and Selected Documents*, 35th Supp. at 98 (1989); United States -- Prohibition of Imports of Tuna and Tuna Products from Canada, *Basic Instruments and Selected Documents*, 29th Supp. at 91 (1983).

encouraged in this manner and rewarded in the international marketplace. Moreover, this dynamic tends to discourage states from internalizing environmental costs rather than encouraging governments to take regulatory action to assure that the prices of manufactured goods reflect the environmental costs associated with them -- a maxim that is well-recognized at the international level as the Polluter-Pays Principle.[7] Equating inadequate environmental policies with export subsidies changes the incentive structure by eliminating the benefits of "race to the bottom" and assures a level playing field for all exporting states.[8]

The actual text of NAFTA, however, contains only one provision that could even remotely be considered an affirmative environmental obligation: article 1114, which very tepidly states that "[t]he Parties recognize that it is inappropriate to encourage investment by relaxing domestic health, safety or environmental measures." Tellingly, this is one of the very few provisions of NAFTA that is expressly unenforceable through the ordinary panel dispute settlement process. By contrast, both the Uruguay Round and NAFTA contain affirmative, minimum standards in the area of intellectual property that have been strongly advocated by the United States. For example, the Uruguay Round requires a minimum 20-year patent term from the date of application[9] by contrast with previous U.S. law, which awarded a patent for 17 years from the date of issue. This provision, which was controversial both internationally and domestically,[10] required a major change in domestic law effected through the Uruguay Round implementing legislation[11] extending the term of U.S. patents. Although one might quibble about the extent to which environmental and public health regulation is analogous to patent protection, the door has certainly been opened wide to the inclusion of affirmative, minimum obligations in international trade agreements.

---

[7] *See, e.g.*, Rio Declaration on Environment and Development, Principle 16, *adopted* June 14, 1992, U.N. Doc. A/CONF.151/5/Rev. 1 (1992), *reprinted in* 31 *I.L.M.* 874 (1992); Recommendation on Guiding Principles Concerning International Economic Aspects of Environmental Policies, O.E.C.D. Doc. C(72)128, *reprinted in* Organisation for Economic Cooperation and Development, *OECD and the Environment* 23 (1986).

[8] *See* Wirth, "The International Trade Regime and the Municipal Law of Federal States: How Close a Fit?" 49 *Wash. & Lee L. Rev.* 1389, 1398-1400 (1992).

[9] Agreement on Trade-Related Aspects of Intellectual Property Rights, Including Trade in Counterfeit Goods, art. 33, *reprinted in* 33 *I.L.M.* 81 (1994).

[10] *See, e.g.*, "Members Urge Clinton Not to Include Patent Changes in Uruguay Round Bill," 11 *Int'l Trade Rep. (BNA)* 1201 (1994).

[11] Uruguay Round Agreements Act s. 532, Pub. L. No. 103-465, 108 Stat. 4809, 4835-36 (1994) (amending 35 U.S.C. s. 154).

3. MULTILATERAL ENVIRONMENTAL AGREEMENTS

Another thorny issue is the relationship between multilateral environmental agreements containing trade measures and international trade agreements. Three principal examples are:

- the Basel Convention on hazardous waste;[12]
- the Convention on International Trade in Endangered Species (CITES);[13] and
- the Montreal Protocol on Substances that Deplete the Ozone Layer.[14]

The entire purpose of the first two of these agreements is to control trade in environmentally sensitive products, and the third utilizes trade measures as an affirmative vehicle to promote the goals of the agreement.

To the extent that these agreements contain measures that are inconsistent with the requirements of trade agreements -- which they almost certainly do -- two GATT panel reports from 1991 and 1994 called their validity into question. To reduce the incidence of death and injury to dolphins snared in tuna fishing operations in the Eastern Tropical Pacific Ocean, U.S. legislation known as the Marine Mammal Protection Act (MMPA)[15] directs the Executive Branch to ban the importation of yellowfin tuna caught by vessels of foreign nations unless there has been a finding that the incidental take of marine mammals is comparable to that of United States vessels. Under the auspices of GATT, Mexico successfully challenged just such a ban on imports of yellowfin tuna from that

---

[12] Basel Convention on the Control of Transboundary Movements of Hazardous Wastes and Their Disposal, March 22, 1989, S. Treaty Doc. No. 5, 102d Cong., 1st Sess. (1991), *reprinted in* 19 *Envtl. Pol'y & L.* 68 (1989), 21 *Int'l Env't Rep. (BNA)* 3101, 28 *I.L.M.* 657 (1989).
[13] Convention on International Trade in Endangered Species (CITES), Mar. 3, 1973, 27 U.S.T. 1087, T.I.A.S. No. 8249, 993 U.N.T.S. 243, *reprinted in* A. Kiss, *Selected Multilateral Treaties in the Field of the Environment* 289 (1983), 21 *Int'l Env't Rep. (BNA)* 2101, 12 *I.L.M.* 1035 (1973).
[14] Montreal Protocol on Substances That Deplete the Ozone Layer, Sept. 16, 1987, S. Treaty Doc. No. 10, 100th Cong., 1st Sess. (1987), *reprinted in* 52 Fed. Reg. 47,515 (Dec. 14, 1987), 17 *Envtl. Pol'y & L.* 256 (1987), 21 *Int'l Env't Rep. (BNA)* 3151, 26 *I.L.M.* 1550 (1987), *adjusted and amended*, June 29, 1990, S. Treaty Doc. No. 4, 102d Cong., 1st Sess. (1991), *reprinted in* 1 *Y.B. Int'l Envtl. L.* 612 (1990), 30 *I.L.M.* 539 (1991), *adjusted and amended*, Nov. 25, 1992, S. Treaty Doc. No. 9, 103d Cong., 1st Sess. (1993), *reprinted in* 32 *I.L.M.* 875 (1993).
[15] Marine Mammal Protection Act of 1972, Pub. L. No. 92-522, s. 101(a)(2), 86 Stat. 1027 (1972), 16 U.S.C. s. 1371(a)(2).

country. The three-member GATT dispute settlement panel concluded among other things that trade measures to protect resources outside the jurisdiction of a GATT party are not permissible.[16] A second successful challenge, initiated by the European Union and the Netherlands, addressed a secondary import ban designed to discourage "tuna laundering" by intermediary nations which purchase yellowfin tuna abroad and export it to the United States and reached a similar conclusion.[17]

Article 104 of NAFTA grandfathers these three agreements by name, but requires consensus among NAFTA parties for inclusion of additional or future multilateral agreements. In effect, then, Mexico and Canada retain unilateral vetoes over future participation by the United States in multilateral environmental agreements with inconsistent trade measures, even those whose parties are virtually universal. The treatment of these agreements in the GATT/World Trade Organization (WTO) system is still unresolved despite several years of debate. One likely possibility, however, is that the WTO will conclude that there is a necessity for a so-called "waiver" of the obligations contained in these agreements under article XXV of the 1947 GATT, which requires the affirmative approval of two-thirds of the WTO member states. This situation raises the serious possibility that the obligations contained in the 1947 GATT might trump trade measures in an international environmental agreement, as is already the case with NAFTA.

In addition, there is the very disturbing possibility that objections from the WTO Secretariat may prevent such measures from being adopted in the first place -- an approach that might be referred to as the "raised eyebrow." For example, during the negotiation of the Montreal Protocol, the GATT Secretariat was consulted about the consistency between the text of the proposed Protocol and that of the GATT. If the GATT Secretariat had identified difficulties with the Protocol's text, those states that were more reluctant, as opposed to more

---

[16] United States -- Restrictions on Imports of Tuna, *Basic Instruments and Selected Documents* 155 (39th Supp. 1993), *reprinted in* 30 *I.L.M.* 1594 (1991).
[17] United States -- Restrictions on Imports of Tuna, *reprinted in* 33 *I.L.M.* 842 (1994). Mexico did not seek the adoption of the first report at the time of its release. However, the GATT Council rejected a request by the European Union to adopt the report. *See* "GATT Council Refuses EC Request to Adopt Panel Report on U.S. Tuna Embargo," 9 *Int'l Trade Rep. (BNA)* 353 (1992). In a discussion of the second report, the GATT Council is reported to have rejected a proposal from the United States that would have opened further Council meetings on that case to the public, and Mexico was said to consider requesting adoption of the first report. Williams, "GATT Shuts Door on Environmentalists," *Financial Times (London)*, July 21, 1994, at 6. As of this writing, neither report has been adopted by the GATT Council and hence neither has yet acquired legal force. *See* Davey, "Dispute Settlement in GATT," 11 *Fordham Int'l L.J.* 51, 94 (1987).

enthusiastic, about reducing emissions of ozone-depleting chemicals would have gained a significant strategic advantage in the negotiations. Alternatively, the trade provisions, which are desirable if not essential contributions to the efficacy of that agreement, might have been excised altogether.

Instead, international environmental agreements that meet certain criteria or have certain attributes ought to be deemed consistent with NAFTA or the GATT. The legal vehicle for reaching this conclusion already exists in the form of article XX of the 1947 GATT text, which exempts certain public health, environmental, and conservation measures from the coverage of that agreement. The criteria employed to determine whether the article XX exceptions are satisfied might include the number of parties to the agreement, the relationship of the trade measures to the goals of the agreement, the urgency of the environmental problem, whether the agreement in question is potentially open to universal membership, and the like.

4. DISTORTIONS FROM THE FAST TRACK PROCESS

Trade agreements such as NAFTA can also disrupt our democratic processes on the national level. In some quarters, including what are commonly considered both "conservative" and "liberal" camps, there have been objections to obligations that constrain or limit governmental authority on the theory that they compromise U.S. sovereignty. This is incorrect, because trade agreements and international institutions created by them, such as the World Trade Organization, are established by a consensual process. Still, the prospect of some loss of freedom in national decision making, whether consensual or not, has been quite troubling.

The domestic status of post-World War II trade agreements in domestic law is somewhat unusual. Congress has the exclusive authority under article I, section 8 of the Constitution to regulate foreign trade. However, under article II, section 2 the President also has the exclusive power to negotiate international agreements with foreign sovereigns. Presumably to dovetail these two functions, after World War II the practice has arisen whereby Congress authorizes the President to negotiate trade agreements by prior statute, within certain broad parameters, on the condition that those agreements not enter into force until given effect by Congress through subsequent implementing legislation. Some have suggested that this "Congressional-Executive" process illegally bypasses the Constitutional requirement for the Senate to give its advice and consent to ratification of treaties by a two-thirds majority,[18] but that appears to be a minority view.

Regardless of the domestic implementation process, the negotiation of trade agreements such as NAFTA is clearly a lawmaking activity, on both the international and national levels. Despite the importance of NAFTA's content both domestically and internationally, Representative Gephardt tellingly described the drafting process as "the most secretive trade negotiations that I have ever monitored,"[19] in which the Executive Branch had virtually sole control. The Executive Branch did not release interim texts of NAFTA. Indeed, when a document purporting to be a draft of the agreement was leaked to the press in late March 1992, the Executive Branch would neither confirm nor deny the authenticity of that document.[20]

One important feature of the domestic process is that the implementing legislation for NAFTA, the GATT Uruguay Round, and other recent trade agreements is adopted under procedures commonly known as the "fast track." Under this procedure, once the implementing legislation is introduced, no amendments are permitted, contrary to ordinary procedure in the Congress. The reason for this is to prevent the Congress from, in effect, renegotiating or undermining the agreement by second-guessing the President's decisions in the negotiation on a case-by-case, individual basis.

Nonetheless, there is a process that duplicates the normal legislative process to a certain extent. Under the fast track procedures, the text of the trade agreement proper is publicly available before Congressional consideration of the domestic legislation for implementing that international instrument. Congress can, and in the case of NAFTA did, hold publicly accessible hearings on the agreement and, by implication, the legislation to implement it as a domestic legal matter. Members of Congress had access on a confidential basis to the draft bill

---

[18] *See* Letter from Laurence H. Tribe, Professor of Law, Harvard University, to Senator Robert Byrd (July 19, 1994), *reprinted in Inside U.S. Trade*, July 22, 1994, at 1 (arguing that "the legal regime put in place by the Uruguay Round represents a structural rearrangement of state-federal relations of the sort that requires ratification by two thirds of the Senate as a Treaty").

[19] Remarks of Representative Richard Gephardt Before the 21st Century Conference, Washington D.C. (Sept. 9, 1994), *reprinted in Fed. News Service*, Sept. 9, 1994 (available in LEXIS, News file).

[20] *See* "Citizen Groups Say Leaked NAFTA Draft Would Undermine U.S. Standards," *Int'l Trade Daily (BNA)*, Mar. 26, 1992. Although there was a dialogue with environmental organizations during the negotiation of the so-called "environmental side agreement" to NAFTA, North American Agreement on Environmental Cooperation, Sept. 8-14, 1993, U.S.-Can.-Mex., *reprinted in* 32 *I.L.M.* 1482 (1993), interim drafts of that instrument also were not released to the public. In any event, the side agreement does not modify the basic NAFTA text.

and even participated in closed "non-markups" and "non-conferences" before it was formally introduced.

Even so, the domestic implementing procedures exacerbated, rather than ameliorated, the lack of public access to the NAFTA negotiation process. The "non-markup" and "non-conference" processes are strictly closed to the public and in practice quite impenetrable. Certain Congressional committees have preferential access to this process. Moreover, the voluminous implementing legislation containing a large number of modifications to domestic U.S. laws was formally released to the public less than two weeks before the House of Representatives voted on the bill on November 17, 1993. Even then, this documentation was not generally available as a practical matter until somewhat later. The Executive Branch released the final version of an environmental analysis of NAFTA to the public a scant four days before the House vote.

Some have defended the fast track process as duplicating all the essential elements of our democratic procedures.[21] Whether or not that might be true in some cases, NAFTA certainly demonstrated the potential for the fast track approach significantly to disrupt the lawmaking process. The fast track process as a whole and the no-amendment rule in particular are purposely designed to affect numerous laws simultaneously and invite a particularly unprincipled sort of horse-trading among issues that would rarely be so closely linked in a typical legislative session, such as the health effects of pesticide residues and intellectual property. Add in the closed nature of the negotiating process, and one truly arrives at "government by trade agreement," characterized by an aggrandizement of Executive prerogatives to a much greater extent than in any other area of domestic law.

Even if the no-amendment rule were to be retained, there are significant opportunities for improving public access to both the negotiation and domestic implementation of future trade agreements. For instance, future legislation authorizing the negotiation of subsequent trade agreements might require that successive interim drafts of any such agreement be made available to the public. Although those procedures are specifically applicable to "treaties and international conventions or agreements,"[22] the National Environmental Policy Act's requirement for preparation of an environmental impact statement (EIS)[23] were

---

[21]   *See, e.g.*, Koh, "The Fast Track and United States Policy," 18 *Brooklyn J. Int'l L.* 143 (1992).
[22]   40 C.F.R. s. 1508.18(b)(1).
[23]   42 U.S.C. s. 4332(C).

held by the D.C. Circuit to be inapplicable to the negotiation of,[24] and adoption of implementing legislation for,[25] NAFTA. Legislation specifically providing for the preparation of an EIS for future trade agreements at both stages would not only facilitate improved governmental decision making with respect to the environmental aspects of the agreement, but would also serve the larger salutary process of improving public participation in the formulation and implementation of the agreement and it implementing legislation.

5. PUBLIC PARTICIPATION IN DISPUTE SETTLEMENT

Another serious issue on both the domestic and international levels concerns public participation in dispute settlement under NAFTA and other trade agreements. The history of the tuna dolphin dispute with Mexico in the GATT, whose dispute settlement procedures are very similar to NAFTA's, is a good example of the need for reform in this area.

As briefly discussed above, this dispute involved a provision of the Marine Mammal Protection Act (MMPA),[26] a statute enacted in 1972 and amended in major respects in 1984[27] and 1988,[28] but never fully implemented by the Executive Branch. The statute in essence requires that the kill of dolphin by foreign fleets incidental to fishing for yellowfin tuna with "purse-seine" nets be commensurate with that of the United States fleet. The remedy for not meeting this standard is trade restrictions on imports of tuna from the offending country. The Earth Island Institute and the Marine Mammal Fund, two private nonprofit organizations, sued in the United States District Court for the Northern District of California under a theory of judicial review and obtained a court order directing the Executive Branch to carry out its nondiscretionary duties under the MMPA by imposing a ban on imports of yellowfin tuna from Mexico and other

---

[24] *Public Citizen v. Office of the United States Trade Representative*, 970 F.2d 916 (D.C. Cir. 1992).

[25] *Public Citizen v. Office of the United States Trade Representative*, 5 F.3d 549 (D.C. Cir. 1993), *cert. denied*, 114 S. Ct. 685 (1994).

[26] 16 U.S.C. s. 1371. The House of Representatives held four days of public hearings on the bill that subsequently became the MMPA. *See* H.R. Rep. No. 702, 92d Cong., 2d Sess. (1972), *reprinted in* 1972 *U.S. Code Cong. & Admin. News* 4144, 4145.

[27] Pub. L. No. 98-364, s. 101, 98 Stat. 440 (1984). *See* H.R. Rep. No. 758, 98th Cong., 2d Sess. 6 (1984), *reprinted in* 1984 *U.S. Code Cong. & Admin. News* 635, 639.

[28] Marine Mammal Protection Act Amendments of 1988, Pub. L. No. 100-711, s. 4, 102 Stat. 4755 (1984). *See* H.R. Rep. No. 970, 100th Cong., 2d Sess. 14-19 (1984), *reprinted in* 1988 *U.S. Code Cong. & Admin. News* 6154, 6155-59.

countries.[29] The Executive Branch then applied an administrative regulation[30] promulgated by the National Oceanic and Atmospheric Administration (NOAA), located in the Department of Commerce, and adopted after publication of a proposed rule and an opportunity for public comment.[31] Relying on that regulation, NOAA made a finding that Mexico had satisfied the statutory standard and lifted the import prohibition. Subsequently, the District Court issued a second order reaffirming the ban after concluding that the regulation was inconsistent with the MMPA and therefore illegal. On appeal, the United States Court of Appeals for the Ninth Circuit affirmed both orders of the District Court.[32]

Mexico initiated a dispute settlement process in GATT, challenging the import ban as a non-tariff barrier to trade. In contrast to the opportunities for public input into the judicial fora in which this dispute was treated on the domestic level, but consistent with standard GATT procedures, the documents and oral proceedings in the case were not accessible to the public.[33] Dispute settlement in GATT does not provide for participation by private parties as intervenors or *amici*. The Earth Island Institute's lawyer, who had initiated the case at the domestic level, travelled to Geneva for the oral proceedings before the panel, but was compelled to wait in the corridor while the panel heard arguments from representatives of the governments of Mexico and the United States.

In this proceeding, however, ten other GATT parties and the European Economic Community made written submissions to the panel, all of which were critical of the MMPA ban and most of which argued that that action is inconsist-

---

[29] *Earth Island Institute v. Mosbacher*, 746 F. Supp. 964 (N.D. Cal. 1990), *aff'd*, 929 F.2d 1449 (9th Cir. 1991).

[30] 50 C.F.R. s. 216.24(e)(5)(iv)-(ix); 55 Fed. Reg. 11,929 (Mar. 30, 1990).

[31] NOAA initially published a proposed rule to implement the 1984 amendments on August 13, 1986. 51 Fed. Reg. 28,963 (Aug. 13, 1986). The comment period on this proposal was subsequently extended, in particular to give potentially affected foreign nations a full opportunity to comment. 51 Fed. Reg. 36,568 (Oct. 14, 1986). NOAA then published an interim final rule in 1988. 53 Fed. Reg. 8911 (Mar. 18, 1988). A second interim final rule with a request for comments, necessitated by the intervening amendments to the MMPA enacted in 1988, was promulgated in 1989. 54 Fed. Reg. 9438 (Mar. 7, 1989). The final regulation published in March 1990 reflected comments on the 1989 interim final rule.

[32] *Earth Island Institute v. Mosbacher*, 929 F.2d 1449 (9th Cir. 1991).

[33] *See, e.g.*, Understanding Regarding Notification, Consultation, Dispute Settlement and Surveillance, Annex para. 6(iv), *Basic Instruments and Selected Documents*, 26th Supp. at 210 (1980) ("Written memoranda submitted to the panel have been considered confidential, but are made available to the parties to the dispute.") *See also* Decision on Improvements to the GATT Dispute Settlement Rules and Procedures, *reprinted in Basic Instruments and Selected Documents*, 36th Supp. at 61 (1990), *reprinted in* 28 *I.L.M.* 1031 (1989) (referencing suggested working procedures establishing that submissions of parties to panels confidential and panel sessions closed).

ent with the GATT. No other contracting parties to the GATT sided with the United States. Further, the United States was represented in the GATT dispute settlement process by the Executive Branch, which had flouted three statutory directives, adopted an illegal regulation, and reluctantly implemented the import ban only under court order. Particularly against the background of the closed nature of the GATT process, questions as to whether the Executive Branch vigorously defended the validity of the ban naturally arose. The inaccessibility of the proceedings to members of the public strongly suggests that important perspectives were not adequately presented to the GATT dispute settlement panel, at least as a formal matter. Although the Executive Branch solicited some input from certain members of the public in the preparation of its submission,[34] those views at most affected only the United States submission to the panel, which in any event must reflect the Government's position. While helpful, that practice is not a substitute for opportunities for written and oral submissions directly to dispute settlement panel.

In short, the many entry points for the public in implementing and adjudicating law on the national level are duplicated poorly if at all in the international trade regime. And, as more and more domestic regulatory issues are taken up in an international trade setting, example of these divergences will very likely increase in number and frequency. The Uruguay Round relaxes the confidentiality requirements for the dispute settlement process somewhat,[35] but NAFTA does not reflect this even this newly-established, although still unsatisfactory, "good practice standard."[36] Under both agreements, there is still a significant potential for the "removal" of a dispute from a domestic to an international forum in which the procedural and participatorial rights of interested private parties are attenuated or eliminated altogether.

---

[34] *See* Letter from Julius L. Katz, Deputy United States Trade Representative, to Justin Ward, Senior Resource Specialist, and Al Meyerhoff, Senior Attorney, Natural Resources Defense Council (Apr. 17, 1992).

[35] *See* Understanding on Rules and Procedures Governing the Settlement of Disputes para. 18.2, 33 *I.L.M.* 112 ("Written submissions to the panel or the [newly created] Appellate Body shall be treated as confidential, but shall be made available to the parties to the dispute. Nothing in this Understanding shall preclude a party to a dispute from disclosing statement [*sic*] of its own positions to the public. Members shall treat as confidential, [*sic*] information submitted by another Member to the panel or the Appellate Body which that Member has designated as confidential. A party to a dispute shall also, upon request of a Member, provide a non-confidential summary of the information contained in its written submissions that could be disclosed to the public.")

[36] *See* North American Free Trade Agreement, *supra* note 1, art. 2012, para. 1(b) ("The panel's hearings, deliberations and initial report, and all written submissions to and communications with the panel shall be confidential.")

It would be entirely feasible to allow private parties to submit additional statements or arguments to dispute settlement panels in a capacity similar to that of *amicus curiae* in domestic law. If *amicus* status could be granted only after submission and approval of a written application, to which the states that are parties to the underlying case could respond, then the panel would have the authority to assure that there is no disruption to the orderly administration of justice. An application might be required to document the applicant's interest, the adequacy of representation of that interest by existing parties, the applicant's potential contribution to a satisfactory resolution of the dispute, the prejudice to the original parties if participation is permitted, and the scope of the proposed submission as *amicus curiae*. If the applicant is permitted to present a written submission, the panel could then decide the additional, distinct question of whether to hear the applicant during oral proceedings. Although as a matter of principle all written submissions to trade agreement dispute settlement panels ought to be available to the public, as a second-best alternative potential *amici* might be requested as a condition of participation to agree to keep documentation submitted by governments confidential. Such proposals, if implemented, can be expected substantially to improve public access to the trade agreement dispute settlement process without disrupting that process.

6. FEDERAL-STATE RELATIONS

Another major structural issue is the effect of NAFTA, the WTO, and the Uruguay Round agreements on state and federal law. These agreements have not just the potential, but the strong likelihood, of disrupting federal-state relationships by "federalizing" issues that were previously the prerogatives of the states.

A report published in 1994 by the European Union[37] emphasizes how much is at stake. That report explicitly targets a number of federal and state-level environmental and public health requirements as non-tariff barriers to trade. Of particular concern are state laws that may have more stringent environmental and public health standards than federal statutes or regulations. Presumably as a consequence, during the debate over the Uruguay Round implementing legislation 44 state attorneys general wrote to the President requesting what they described as a summit meeting on this issue.[38]

Because of concerns such as these, the NAFTA implementing legislation

---

[37] European Union, *Report On United States Barriers To Trade And Investment* (1994).
[38] "State Groups, Lawmakers Oppose Pre-Emption Of State Law Under GATT," 11 *Int'l Trade Rep. (BNA)* 1136 (1994).

established a federal-state consultation process in the event of a challenge by one of the other NAFTA parties to the law of a state or any of its political subdivisions.[39] Ultimately, however, the NAFTA implementing legislation, like that for other trade agreements before it, preserves judicial remedies for federal authorities to sue state governments to compel compliance with trade agreements and actions taken under them.[40] Of course, in a federal state like the United States, there must be a mechanism to assure that subsidiary governmental units such as the states in the United States and the provinces in Canada observe international law. However, the real question is the form of that mechanism, consistent with our notions of federalism and preemption. In the pesticide area, for instance, the states may take certain actions that are more stringent than provided in federal law.[41]

An entirely viable alternative to allowing the Executive Branch to extinguish these rights by judicial action would be to preserve the full autonomy of subsidiary governmental units after the agreement enters into effect. Then, if a problem were to arise concerning implementation at the state or local level, the Executive Branch could negotiate with those bodies. If those negotiations were to fail, special legislation preempting the rights of the state in question on a particular issue could be adopted by Congress, specially tailored to that problem situation. This is yet another area in which trade agreements unnecessarily serve as a vehicle for the expansion of Executive Branch power, in this case at the expense of the states. The inclusion of the Congress in the implementation process is highly desirable an additional forum in which to debate the merits of any adverse dispute settlement panel report and the form of compliance by the United States. Otherwise, we may have no way of even knowing what we are giving up at the sub-national level if virtually any state or local law, regulation, or ordinance can be "federalized" through the avenue of a trade agreement -- again, "government by trade agreement."

7. FEDERAL ADMINISTRATIVE LAW

Trade agreements may also disrupt administrative processes and law at the federal level. Contrary to the assertions of some, it is well established that adverse

---

[39] North American Free Trade Agreement Implementation Act, Pub. L. 103-182, s. 101(b)(1), 107 Stat. 2057 (1993).
[40] *Id.* s. 101(b)(1).
[41] *See, e.g., Wisconsin Public Intervenor v. Mortier*, 501 U.S. 597 (1991); *Coparr, Ltd. v. City of Boulder*, 942 F.2d 724 (10th Cir. 1991).

reports of GATT dispute settlement panels cannot repeal federal statutes. But as any student of administrative law will attest, statutory law is but one component of the regulatory process. Most federal environmental statutes require subsequent implementation through administrative rulemaking or other unilateral Executive Branch action. In this realm of purely Executive prerogative, there may be little or nothing to keep the Executive from unilaterally relaxing a domestic standard in response to an adverse panel report. And because of the "negative" character of trade agreements, the change will always have a weakening effect on the rigor of domestic regulatory requirements.

An excellent example of precisely this phenomenon has recently occurred. Pursuant to the Clean Air Act,[42] the Environmental Protection Agency in early 1994 promulgated rules concerning "reformulated" gasoline, which reduces ground-level ozone in highly polluted areas.[43] Those regulations establish standards for reformulated gasoline as measured against a baseline, the calculation of which is specified in the rules. Domestic refiners are permitted to choose among three methods of calculating this baseline. For reasons related to differences between imported and domestically produced gasoline, however, fewer options are available for establishing the baseline in the case of gasoline produced at foreign refineries. The Venezuelan national oil company protested that the EPA rules discriminate against imported gasoline in contravention of the GATT. Subsequently, EPA in May 1994 published a proposed amendment to its reformulated gasoline regulations to address these complaints.[44] Congress in an appropriations measure subsequently prohibited EPA from finalizing the proposed rule,[45] and Venezuela's challenge to the reformulated gasoline regulations will be the subject of the first dispute settlement panel established under the auspices of the WTO.[46]

Entirely apart from the effect of EPA's proposed amendment on air quality in the United States and the merits of Venezuela's challenge in the WTO, both of which are complex, this situation is revealing for its impact on domestic administrative processes. In such a situation, there is every reason to believe that back-channel negotiations with foreign governments might subvert the integrity of the notice-and-comment rulemaking process and could serve as an invitation to circumvent statutory standards. The House Committee on Energy and Com-

---

[42]   42 U.S.C. s. 7545(k).
[43]   50 C.F.R. s. 80.91-.93; 59 Fed. Reg. 7791 (Feb. 16, 1994).
[44]   59 Fed. Reg. 22,800 (May 3, 1994).
[45]   Pub. L. No. 103-327, 108 Stat. 2299, 2322 (1994).
[46]   *See* Frances Williams, "WTO Sets Up First Disputes Panel," *Financial Times (London)*, Apr. 11, 1995, at 6.

merce, which held hearings on this matter, articulated precisely this concern by observing that "the State Department had made commitments regarding the rule to the Venezuelans which made the public participation requirements of the [Clean Air Act] ineffective."[47]

In such a case, the courts and the institution of judicial review may provide the only meaningful remedy to assure that the Executive Branch satisfies domestic statutory criteria, both substantive and procedural. However, in federal court an issue like the reformulated gasoline rule appears not just as an ordinary regulation in a garden-variety proceeding for judicial review, but also as a foreign relations issue. As anyone who has worked in this area will confirm, the courts are much more deferential to the Executive Branch in a foreign relations setting. In fact, in subsequent judicial proceedings in the tuna dolphin controversy concerning the secondary import ban from tuna processed in intermediary nations, the Executive Branch did not hesitate to emphasize the potential harm to foreign relations if the court were to rule against the Government.[48]

An earlier series of judicial proceedings clearly demonstrates the potential for difficulties when questions of statutory interpretation and the integrity of agency regulatory process appear in a foreign relations context. In the mid-1980s EPA, acting on evidence that the fumigant ethylene dibromide (EDB) causes cancer, genetic mutations, and adverse reproductive effects in human beings, banned that pesticide for use on domestic produce. By contrast, in response to assertions from the Department of State that the ban would damage the economies of friendly exporting countries, EPA promulgated a tolerance permitting that continued to allow residues of 30 parts per billion (ppb) of EDB in imported mangoes. The United States Court of Appeals for the District of Columbia Circuit set aside the tolerance, concluding that because EPA was required by statute to base pesticide residue limitations on health considerations, the agency's reli-

---

[47] H.R. Rep. No. 882, 103d Cong., 2d Sess. (1994), *available in* 1995 WL 14808 at *647-48 (available in Legislative History database).

[48] While the [Executive Branch] did not argue that the court was legally bound by the Panel's decision in interpreting the intermediary embargo nation provisions of the MMPA, the government did go to great lengths to make the court aware of the Panel's decision. Implicit in this effort to present the court with the Panel's decision was the notion that the court should be aware of, and consider in its decision, the effects of its decision on foreign trade relations. The United States pointed to the Panel's decision as evidence of the substantial friction that could result from a more stringent reading of the intermediary nations embargo provisions of the MMPA. R.F. Housman and D. J. Zaelke, "The Collision of the Environment and Trade: The GATT Tuna/Dolphin Decision," 22 *Envtl. L. Rep. (Envtl. L. Inst.)* 10,268 (1992).

ance solely on concerns of foreign affairs was illegal.[49]

On remand, EPA reaffirmed the residue limitation for imported mangoes, but came up with new justifications for that tolerance. The Agency concluded that the special exemption was warranted by ongoing cooperative efforts with food-exporting nations to assure that fruit and vegetables enter the United States free of pests like the Mediterranean fruitfly, diseases, and unsafe levels of pesticides. Moreover, mango-producing nations were channelling export revenues into the search for alternatives for EDB. Accordingly, EPA concluded that revoking the EDB tolerance and prohibiting the importation of contaminated mangoes into the United States would pose greater risks to the food supply than continuing to allow the entry of the pesticide-laced produce. To put it kindly, this reasoning is counterintuitive. Nonetheless, after EPA provided assurances with respect to the limited term of the standard for imported mangoes, the Court of Appeals, accepting this rationalization, approved the very same tolerance that that court had earlier set aside as a violation of the statutory standard.[50] Although the D.C. Circuit's second review of the mango tolerance was phrased as a pure question of statutory interpretation of the health-based standard in the governing statute, the court could hardly have been deaf to the Government's clear assertions of harm to foreign relations.

As in the case of state laws, this "internationalization" of federal law is not a healthy thing for democratic decision making processes. Moreover, this situation could easily be corrected by an express statement in the domestic implementing legislation establishing that the conclusions of dispute settlement panel reports shall be without legal effect in administrative or judicial proceedings. Without such guarantees, there is a significant likelihood that the Executive Branch can act unilaterally with few if any restrictions, either from the legislative or judicial branches, in areas of domestic jurisdiction that happen to fall within the purview of international trade agreements -- again, "government by trade agreement." The proposed reform, moreover, is entirely consistent with the principle that dispute settlement panel reports have no domestic legal effect. Of course, Congress could still act to overturn a regulation that did not conform to the expectations of a dispute settlement panel constituted under an international trade agreement. That check, however, is highly desirable to assure multi-branch action on behalf of the United States Government and to guarantee adequate public access

---

[49] *Nat'l Coalition Against the Misuse of Pesticides v. Thomas*, 809 F.2d 875 (D.C. Cir. 1987).
[50] *Nat'l Coalition Against the Misuse of Pesticides v. Thomas*, 815 F.2d 1579 (D.C. Cir. 1987).

to domestic decision making processes in areas affected by the actions of multi-lateral trade bodies.

8. CONCLUSION

This chapter is not an argument against NAFTA or international trade agreements more generally. Instead, it is a plea for a sense of proportion or perspective concerning the importance of liberalized trade by comparison with other social welfare concerns, such as environment and public health. Significantly, every one of the problems identified here can be solved, or at least ameliorated, through sound choices in negotiating future trade agreements and in drafting their implementing legislation. In that regard, we would be wise to continue to heed the words of Benjamin Disraeli who, more than a century and a half ago, remarked that "[f]ree trade is not a principle; it is an expedient."[51] That observation is as valid today as it was then.

---

[51] Speech on Import Duties (Apr. 25, 1843).

Chapter Seven

NAFTA REVISITED

by Dorinda G. Dallmeyer

1. INTRODUCTION

Where has NAFTA gotten Canada, Mexico, and the United States since its implementation in 1994? This concluding chapter covers the events over the two years since NAFTA's implementation began. Because each country has distinct cultural identity problems, this chapter opens with an examination of developments in cultural identity issues. It then examines the effects NAFTA has had on economic and trade concerns among the member states. In addressing developments regarding environmental protection, we will learn that this forum has led to some new innovations in the area of resolution of disputes. The chapter closes with an evaluation of the prospects for accession of new members to NAFTA.

2. CULTURAL IDENTITY

Beginning a new phase of what one commentator called a return to "nativism and legalism,"[1] immigration reform in the United States became a reality in 1996 when Congress passed and the President signed into law new restrictions on immigration. Coupled with welfare restrictions signed in August, the immigration bill makes illegal immigrants ineligible for most public assistance pro-

---

[1]   Rosen, "Why the Courts Can't Save Us: The War on Immigrants," *New Republic*, Jan. 30, 1995, at 22.

D. G. Dallmeyer (ed.), Joining Together, Standing Apart: National Identities after NAFTA, 131–148.
© 1997 *Kluwer Law International. Printed in the Netherlands.*

grams financed by the Federal government and states.[2] It speeds up determinations on claims for asylum, with the hearing required to take place within seven days after the request and no additional appeals on asylum denials.[3] The new law also severely limits the ability of non-citizens to file class action suits regarding immigration and naturalization procedures. In fact the Justice Department has already gone to federal court seeking the dismissal of four of the five class action suits presently before the courts, affecting the status of hundreds of thousands of aliens who are challenging Immigration and Naturalization Service decisions regarding eligibility for legal residence.[4]

[2]   Branigan, "Immigration: Focus is Borders, Not Benefits," Wash. Post, Oct. 1, 1996, at A1; "Education Clause Delays Illegal Immigration Bill," *id.*, Aug. 3, 1996, at A4; "Punishing Legal Immigrants," *id.*, Sept. 27, 1996, at A24.; "Inflating Immigration Figures", *id.*, Dec. 2, 1996, at A20. For an analysis of one state's approach to curbing illegal immigration, see "Wilson Signs Order Curbing Benefits for Illegal Immigrants," *id.*, Aug. 28, 1996, at A6 (California).
[3]   "Restricting Immigrants: The Details," N.Y. Times, Oct. 1, 1996, at A22. The new law also will double the number of border patrol agents by the year 2001 and will add 2700 detention cells. Additionally, prison terms for smuggling people into the United States and for the use of fraudulent government identification documents were increased sharply.
[4]   Johnston, "Government is Quick to Use Power of Immigration Law," N.Y. Times, Oct. 22, 1996, at A16.

Hand in hand with the new immigration laws, the new welfare law bars legal immigrants, as well as most permanent residents and refugees granted asylum, from receiving welfare and Medicaid benefits during their first five years in the country, as well as denying them food stamps and supplemental security income assistance to the disabled and the elderly.[5] The changes are estimated to affect approximately 900,000 eligible for food stamps and over 500,000 receiving supplemental security benefits.

To the north, Canada struggled not with immigrants but with the longstanding problem of how to accommodate its Francophone heritage. For the second time in 15 years, Canada faced a separatist referendum in Quebec in 1995. The vote was extremely close, 50.6 percent against secession and 49.4 percent in favor.[6] The *Parti Québécois* may mount another referendum as soon as 1997. Although the referendum is for political separation, the secessionists wish to remain economically integrated with Canada. While the vote represented a narrow defeat for the secessionists, the closeness of the margin may provide Quebec with additional leverage to force concessions from Ottawa to ensure greater autonomy and power for the province. Should a secessionist referendum ever succeed, the province might decide to negotiate with the national government, excluding other provinces from the negotiations. Experts fear this choice in turn would trigger similar secessionist moves in Ontario and the western provinces. Another scenario envisions that Ottawa and Ontario agree to the split and form something resembling the European Community, with the provinces holding political autonomy while remaining economically interdependent. Of course, this path would not address the concerns of other provinces, who may then turn to pursuing independence for themselves.

---

[5] Soros, "Immigrants' Burden," N.Y. Times, Oct. 2, 1996, at A15. *See also* Kleinfeld, "New Law Is Sowing Fear and Confusion at Nation's Welfare Offices," *id.*, Sept. 26, 1996, at A17; Pear, "For Legal Immigrants, a Welfare Reprieve," *id.*, Oct. 3, 1996, at A21. For a highly critical analysis of the immigration reform bill, see Judis, "Huddled Elites," *New Republic*, Dec. 23, 1996, at 25.

[6] *See* "Why Canada Will Remain United," 4 *Canada Q.* 1-2 (Oct. 1996) (address by Stéphan Dion, President of the Privy Council and Minister of Intergovernmental Affairs); "Canada Tries to Get Back On Track after Defeat of Quebec Sovereignty," 12 *Int'l Trade Rep. (BNA)* 1805-1806 (Nov. 1, 1995); "Neuchterlein Discusses Canada's Future," 12 *Miller Center Rep.* 8-9 (Spring 1996); "Provinces Will Omit Separate Quebec from Canada's Internal Trade Accord," 12 *Int'l Trade Rep. (BNA)* 1487-1488 (Sept. 6, 1995)(implications for NAFTA); "Independent Quebec Group Pushes Trade; Firms Worry about Separation's Effect," *id.* 1608 (Sept. 27, 1995); "Independent Quebec's Access to WTO, NAFTA is Not a Given, Minister Warns," *id.* 1644-1645 (Oct. 4, 1995). For a description of U.S. congressional hearings on the potential effects of Quebec secession, see DePalma, "For Canada, Is U.S. Gaze Offensive or Friendly?," N.Y. Times, Sept. 26, 1996, at 4.

In view of the chaos and uncertainty such a secessionist success could bring, Canada's Attorney General in September 1996 asked the Supreme Court for a declaration on the legality of a unilateral declaration of independence.[7] The announcement brought an immediate outcry from *Parti Québécois* separatists, who pointed out that the Supreme Court should have nothing to rule on because the Canadian Constitution does not mention any rules of separation. Even if it did, the Province of Quebec does not recognize the Constitution as binding.[8]

Despite polls which show 57 percent of Quebec residents do not want to repeat the referendum process within the next decade,[9] political pressure has been growing to reinvigorate enforcement of Quebec's language regulations. For example, a proposed law before the provincial government would forbid the sale of video games or computer software in English if a French language version is available anywhere in the world. Another would return "language inspectors" to patrol businesses to ensure French was being used, despite a finding by the United Nations Human Rights Commission that the language law is a violation of the International Covenant on Civil and Political Rights.[10] Domestically, over the last 20 years, the uncertainty created by this seesaw battle over separation and sovereignty has contributed to the exodus of more than 300,000 English-speakers as well as the relocation of over 1000 companies from the province.[11]

While balancing its intramural cultural battles, the Canadian government doggedly continued attempts to protect the country from further incursions by American culture, a policy dating back to the 1960s. Among the NAFTA parties, only Canada made cultural protection a high priority and gained exemptions to protect its cultural identity.[12]

The problem with Canada's cultural protection policy is in distinguishing between what constitutes an appropriate measure to guard Canadian culture versus what constitutes an unfair trade practice. This time the dilemma emerged in the form of an excise tax Canada imposed on so-called "split-run" magazines, i.e., American magazines marketed in Canada with some Canadian content

---

[7] "Canada Asks Top Court For Ruling On Secession," N.Y. Times, Sept. 26, 1996, at A7.

[8] *Id.*

[9] DePalma, "In Quebec, A Self-Fulfilling Separatism," N.Y. Times, Oct. 20, 1996, at E4.

[10] Trueheart, "Quebec 'Language Police' to Resume Enforced Use of French," Wash. Post, July 14, 1996, at A23.

[11] DePalma, *supra* note 9.

[12] DePalma, "Trade v. Cultural Identity in Canada," N.Y. Times, Oct. 7, 1996, at C9.

(although U.S. content predominates) and with Canadian advertising.[13] Beginning in 1995, Canada imposed an 80 percent excise tax on the total dollar value of the Canadian advertising in split-run magazines as a way to reserve the small pool of Canadian advertising dollars available to Canadian publications, thereby protecting indigenous publishers from having to compete with U.S. entertainment giants. The tax was seen as a way to forestall the entry of over 120 U.S. magazines and trade journals that a Canadian task force identified as contemplating the creation of split-run editions.[14]

Although the United States and Canada have engaged in informal talks over the decades regarding Canadian cultural protection, and although the Chapter 20 review process under NAFTA remained an optional forum for the dispute, the United States chose instead to file a formal complaint before the World Trade Organization; in doing so it cleverly bypassed the NAFTA dispute resolution process entirely.[15] Along with the split-run tax issue, the United States included in its filing complaints regarding preferential postal rates for Canadian magazines and a ban on the importation of Canadian editions printed in the United States, a practice which dates back 30 years. The WTO ruled against Canada in March 1997; Canada intends to appeal.[16]

Rather than a focus on external factors as a problem in cultural identity, the culture clash typifying Mexico over the past two years has been the continuing confrontation presented by the Zapatista rebels in the state of Chiapas to the federal government.[17] The "rebellion," launched the same day as the entry into force of NAFTA, led the Mexican government to engage in negotiations with the

---

[13] "Canada Will Proceed with Taxation on Split-Run Magazines, Dupuy Says," 12 *Int'l Trade Rep. (BNA)* 1605 (Sept. 27, 1995).

[14] *See* DePalma, *supra* note 12.

[15] "Canadian Academic Questions Wisdom of Cultural Exemption under NAFTA," 12 *Int'l Trade Rep. (BNA)* 1778-1779 (Oct. 25, 1995); "Kantor says U.S. Is Examining Options to Respond to Canadian Split-Run Tax," *id.* 2101-2102 (Dec. 20, 1995); "Kantor Asks for Consultations on Canadian Split-Run Tax Dispute," 13 *Int'l Trade Rep. (BNA)* 420-421 (Mar. 13, 1996); "U.S. Initiates WTO Case over Canadian Split-Run Policies, Postal Rates," *Inside U.S. Trade* (Mar. 15, 1996); "U.S. Requests WTO Panel to Probe Canadian Split-Run Magazine Taxes," 13 *Int'l Trade Rep. (BNA)* 978 (June 12, 1996). More than 450 U.S. magazines are sold in Canada; 80% of all English-language publications available on Canadian newsstands are imported, and of those, 90% come from the United States.

[16] "Canada to Appeal WTO Ruling on Magazine Tax, Eggleton Says," 14 *Int'l Trade Rep. (BNA)* 520-521 (Mar. 19, 1997).

[17] For a description of international involvement with the Zapatista negotiations, see Preston, "Zapatista Tour Offers Mud, Sweat and Radical Chic," N.Y. Times, Aug. 13, 1996, at A5.

Zapatistas. Despite the government's statements that indicated it wished a peaceful settlement, over the last two years government negotiators frequently have suspended talks and, rather than putting forth new proposals, simply recycled PRI rhetoric. Indeed during the summer of 1996, the government's representatives rejected several demands found in a Zapatista position paper; it turned out that among the paragraphs bracketed as objectionable by the government were two articles taken directly from the Mexican Federal Constitution. [18] Government proposals for electoral reform failed to address other issues important to the Zapatistas such as permitting independent candidates to run for office outside the traditional party structures, access to the media, campaign financing, autonomy for electoral institutions, and procedures for impeachment of public officials. Additionally, the military presence has remained quite strong in Chiapas.

Complicating the negotiations was the emergence of another rebel group, the EPR or PRA depending on the acronym in English or Spanish.[19] Through 18 coordinated surprise attacks at army installations and police stations across six Mexican states in late August 1996, the PRA left 16 dead and claimed to have begun a revolution that would bring in a revolutionary socialist government. The Zapatistas sought immediately to distance themselves from the PRA, declining any support from them and noting "You fight to seize power, We fight for

[18] Letter from Alejandro Nadal to the author (Aug. 28, 1996). *See also* Preston, "Zapatistas Suspend Talks In a Rebuff to Zedillo," N.Y. Times, Sept. 4, 1996, at A4; "A Risky New Role for Mexico's Army," *id.*, Oct. 20, 1996, at E14.

Although negotiations between the government and the Zapatistas remain in suspension, there was a flurry of activity in mid-October 1996 to negotiate the visit of "Commander Ramona" to attend the National Indian Conference in Mexico City. The government apparently feared her presence could cause public disturbances either supporting or opposing the Zapatistas, yet her appearance had little impact outside the conference. *See* Preston, "Dying Zapatista Leader is Focus of Only Accord So Far," N.Y. Times, Oct. 11, 1996, at A3; Preston, "A Dying Chief of Zapatistas in Mexico City," *id.*, Oct. 13, 1996, at 7. For an analysis of how all three NAFTA members cope with indigenous peoples, see DePalma, "Three Countries Face Their Indians," N.Y. Times, Dec. 15, 1996, at E3. The Organization of American States finally was allowed into Mexico for the first time in 1996 to examine human rights abuses against indigenous groups. *See* Dillon, "O.A.S. Rights Group Is Told of Abuses on Visit to Mexico," *id.*, July 25, 1996, at A5.

[19] *See* Preston, "Mexican Group Displays Rebel Credentials," N.Y. Times, Aug. 10, 1996, at 5; Dillon, "Rebels Strike in 4 Mexico States, Leaving 13 Dead," *id.*, Aug. 30, 1996, at A1; Dillon, "In Mexico, Rebels Evoke Mixed Feelings," *id.*, Aug. 31, 1996, at 5; Dillon, "Mexicans Trace Rebels' History," *id.*, Sept. 5, 1996, at A1; Preston, "Mexico's Army Out of the Barracks," *id.*, Sept. 14, 1996, at 5; Dillon, "The Rebels' Call to Arms Echoes in Rural Mexico," *id.*, Sept. 19, 1996, at A3; "Raid by Mexican Forces Seizes 11 as Guerillas," *id.*, Sept. 28, 1996, at 7; Preston, "For Mexicans in a Violent, Backward Area, a Quiet Election," *id.*, Oct. 7, 1996, at A6; Preston, "Mexico's Wary Crackdown on Rebels," *id.*, Oct. 16, 1996, at A9.

democracy, liberty, and justice. It's not the same."[20] Likewise the PRA apparently disdains the Zapatista decision to negotiate with the government at all. Despite the Zapatista decision to walk out of the talks with the government in the fall of 1996, President Zedillo also distinguished the Zapatistas from the PRA, calling the PRA terrorists, and expressing hopes that the Zapatistas would return to the bargaining table.[21] As for the PRA, the Government initiated a massive effort to round up PRA rebels in six southern states and, for the most part, the PRA attacks have subsided.[22]

3. TRADE AND ECONOMICS

If NAFTA was alternately painted by its supporters as paradise and by its detractors as perdition, the truth lies somewhere in between. It remains difficult to measure the economic impact of NAFTA, for the provisions of the agreement hardly can be evaluated in isolation from other factors, particularly the collateral effects of the Mexican peso crisis. NAFTA did the obvious in terms of its basic aim: the reduction or elimination of tariffs did increase the flow of goods among the member countries.[23] Indeed, for 1994-1995, U.S. merchandise exports to Mexico increased by 22 percent and U.S. merchandise imports from Mexico increased 26 percent.[24] Devaluation of the peso, however, caused U.S. goods to become more expensive in Mexico than Mexican goods; consequently, by January 1996 Mexico posted a record trade surplus with the United States of $779 million.[25] Yet it would be misleading to ascribe the trade surplus to the creation of NAFTA; more accurately the effects are due to the peso devaluation and the existence of trade with Mexico, regardless of the presence of NAFTA.

Another related fear at NAFTA's inception was potential job flight from the United States and Canada to Mexico. Many NAFTA opponents warned that

---

[20] Preston, "Zapatistas Suspend Talks In a Rebuff To Zedillo," N.Y. Times, Sept. 4, 1996, at A4 (quoting Subcommander Marcos, the Zapatista's main strategist).
[21] Preston, "Stung by Attacks, Mexico Intensifies Search for Rebels," N.Y. Times, Aug. 31, 1996, at 1.
[22] "Mexican Rebels Declare Truce in Southern State," N.Y. Times, Sept. 26, 1996, at A7 (month-long ceasefire prior to national elections).
[23] *See* Gonzalez, "The North American Free Trade Agreement," 30 *Int'l Law.* 345-366, 352 (1996).
[24] *Id.* at 351. U.S. merchandise exports to Mexico rose 27% between Sept. 1995 and Sept. 1996, while U.S. consumer goods were up 37% over the same period. *See* 6 *Clearinghouse on State Int'l Policies* 1-2 (Nov.-Dec. 1996).
[25] *See* Gonzalez, *supra* note 23, at 351.

businesses would move south, attracted by cheap labor and lax regulatory enforcement. The peso crisis played a role here as well, because anxiety about the stability of the Mexican government and currency possibly stemmed relocation to Mexico and discouraged foreign direct investment.[26] According to figures compiled by the U.S. Department of Labor in late 1995, the NAFTA Transitional Adjustment Assistance program had certified 42,221 workers eligible to receive assistance under the program. Of the 317 petitions certified by that date, 139 involved shifts in production to Mexico and 47 shifts in production to Canada. The remainder were attributed to increased imports, either by companies or customers, from Canada (57 instances) or Mexico (42 instances).[27] Thirty-two petitions failed to specify which country was the source of competing imports. Similarly, Canada reported the loss of about 850 auto jobs to Mexico.[28] In comparison, one commentator ascribed the loss of 1 million Mexican jobs to the peso crisis.[29] Yet another study released in late 1996 reported that jobs created in the United States to serve the export market only slightly edged out the number of jobs lost by the United States to Mexico and Canada.[30]

---

[26] Sanger, "Mexico Says It Will Repay $7 Billion To the U.S.," N.Y. Times, July 26, 1996, at C1, C5. It is worth noting that although wages may be lower in Mexico, benefits are more extensive. Mexican workers are granted more paid vacation time, higher overtime rates, an easier path to unionization, and receive mandatory profit-sharing. *See* "Mexico's Lower Wages Are Countered by Higher Benefit Costs," 12 *Int'l Trade Rep. (BNA)* 1723-1724 (Oct. 18, 1995).

[27] "DOL Statistics Show Significant Increase in Workers Losing Jobs Because of NAFTA," 12 *Int'l Trade Rep. (BNA)* 1862 (Nov. 8, 1995). There have been disparate impacts for NAFTA-related job loss. According to a study by the Institute for Policy Studies, rural communities have suffered more than urban areas. Also NAFTA has had a disproportionate impact on women because of their concentration in the apparel and electronics industries, the two sectors with the highest rates of NAFTA-related layoffs. For a description of the Institute's findings, see "Study Says NAFTA-Related Job Losses Particularly High in Rural Areas," *id.* 1933 (Nov. 22, 1995). In comparison, the U.S. textile manufacturing sector has been able to hold the line against job flight by increasing their supplies of textiles to factories in the western hemisphere. *See* Holusha, "Squeezing the Textile Workers," N.Y. Times, Feb. 21, 1996, at C1, C6.

[28] "NAFTA Plant Closings," 13 *Int'l Trade Rep. (BNA)* 655 (Apr. 17, 1996).

[29] "Mexican Workers Pay the Price of U.S. Bailout," N.Y. Times, Sept. 30, 1996, at A14.

[30] Stevenson, "Nafta's Impact on Jobs Has Been Slight, Study Says," N.Y. Times, Dec. 19, 1996, at C1, C3. Although the net gain is very small, there was a great deal of fluctuation in job losses and gains. The study focused primarily on Mexico and found that the peso crisis was far more influential on jobs than was NAFTA. For other views on NAFTA's impact, see "NAFTA, U.S. Companies Fail to Deliver Jobs, Exports, Report Says," *Inside U.S. Trade* (Sept. 8, 1995); Herbert, "Nafta's Bubble Bursts," N.Y. Times, Sept. 11, 1995, at A11; Tollerson, "Perot, in Video Lecture, Renews Attack on Trade Accord," *id.*, Sept. 16, 1996, at A11.

Things to look FOR AFTER NAFTA

Royal Canadian
Mounted Migrant
Worker

Air Hernandez
Basketball Shoes

Driver's side
Pinata

Reprinted by permission of Dr. Brian Moench and In Your Face Cards.

An interesting result of the focus on job volatility has been the increase of coordinated union activity across borders, both in organizing workers and in bringing complaints of unfair labor practices to the attention of the NAFTA governing authorities.[31] Under the North American Agreement on Labor Cooperation, each NAFTA member sets up its own National Administrative Office (NAO) to investigate allegations of a failure by NAFTA members to enforce labor laws. Using this process, American unions have challenged labor practices in Mexico and vice versa.[32] While the unions have had mixed success, the experience thus far indicates that there may be procedural problems (particularly in Mexico) in ensuring that the NAO process is free of the appearance of governmental interference.[33] Also, the NAOs are limited to making findings and recommendations and cannot issue enforcement decrees. In light of these limita-

---

[31] Goldberg, "U.S. Labor Makes Use of a Trade Accord It Has Opposed," N.Y. Times, Feb. 28, 1996, at A14; Greitzer, "Cross-Border Responses to Labor Repression in North America," 1995 *Det. C.L. Mich. St. U. L. Rev.* 917-971.

[32] For example, Mexican telephone workers challenged a decision by Sprint Corp. to terminate 235 workers in San Francisco who staffed its Spanish-speaking subsidiary, La Conexion Familiar. The Mexican union alleged the workers were dismissed for trying to unionize, rather than Sprint's claim that it was solely a business decision. *See* "Telephone Workers Union of Mexico Files Charge Against Sprint Under NAFTA," 12 *Int'l Trade Rep. (BNA)* 307 (Feb. 15, 1995); "U.S. Reviews Mexican NAO Request to Discuss Sprint Labor Practices," *id.* 989-990 (June 7, 1995); "Union Leaders in Mexico Meet with Labor Secretary on Sprint Case," *id.* 1141 (July 5, 1995); "U.S., Mexico Accord on Sprint Calls for Study of Plant Closings," *id.* 2104-2105 (Dec. 20, 1995); "Public Hearing on Sprint Charges Set for Feb. 27 in San Francisco," 13 *Int'l Trade Rep. (BNA)* 152-153 (Jan. 31, 1996); "NLRA Failed to Protect Sprint Workers, Union Tells NAFTA Trilateral Committee," *id.* 373-374 (Mar. 6, 1996).
In another incident, the U.S. NAO found obstruction of the unionization process at a Sony plant in Mexico in a complaint brought before it by four U.S. and Mexican human rights organizations. However, only the Mexican government could order Sony to rehire the workers. *See* "Mexico Union Registration Process Faulted in U.S. NAO Report on Sony," 12 *Int'l Trade Rep. (BNA)* 696-698 (Apr. 19, 1995). Members of the United Electrical Workers withdrew their complaint regarding failure to enforce Mexican labor laws regarding unionization of a GE plant there, calling the investigation a "whitewash." One of the problems cited was the decision of the NAO to hold the hearings 550 miles away from the workers. *See* "Electrical Workers Drops GE Petition, Calling NAO Mexico Probe A 'Whitewash,'" *id.* 272 (Feb. 8, 1995). However, another probe related to electronics remains pending before the U.S. NAO. *See* "CWA Charges in NAFTA Complaint Mexico Failed to Protect Union Activists," 13 *Int'l Trade Rep. (BNA)* 1584-1586 (Nov. 16, 1996). And the U.S. NAO is looking into allegations that Mexican government workers were impaired in their ability to organize. *See* "U.S. NAO Sets NAFTA Hearing On Charge Concerning Mexican Government Workers," *id.* 1717 (Nov. 6, 1996).

[33] *See* "First Three Years of NAFTA Show Need for Renegotiation, Groups Say," 13 *Int'l Trade Rep. (BNA)* 1867-1868 (Dec. 4, 1996)(report prepared by the Institute for Policy Studies and the International Labor Rights Fund).

tions, there have been calls for renegotiation of the side accord not only to increase the NAOs' clout but to address root causes of labor/management inequality.[34]

Despite Congressional warnings to the contrary in 1995, in January 1997 the Mexican government repaid all of the US$12.5 billion loan, not only with interest, but also three years ahead of schedule.[35] With the peso crisis finally out of the way, we now may be able to begin to gather statistics on NAFTA's effect on trade, jobs, and economics without the bias of a currency system gone awry.

4. ENVIRONMENT

Although the initial impetus for the environmental side agreement may have come from fears that Mexico would use lax enforcement of its environmental laws to attract business, in practice the dispute resolution mechanism has been invoked against all three member states. However, thus far, only activities occurring in Mexico have proceeded beyond the initial stages of the process. The North American Council on Environmental Cooperation (NACEC) refused to review U.S. congressional decisions to rescind a portion of funding for the Fish and Wildlife Service and to expedite salvage logging in U.S. national forests by suspending the Endangered Species Act.[36] It also declined to proceed with a complaint regarding an alleged failure by Canada and the province of Alberta to enforce environmental laws which resulted in the pollution of wetlands and harm to fish and migratory birds.[37]

---

[34] *Id.* The report specifically recommends changing the tribunals that are required to register unions.

[35] *See* Sanger, "Mexico Pays Off U.S. Loans 3 Years Ahead of Schedule," N.Y. Times, Jan. 16, 1997, at A1, C8. *See also* Friedman, "The Critics Were Wrong," *id.*, Sept. 25, 1996, at A19.

[36] For discussions of the Endangered Species Act complaint, see Submission on Enforcement Matter, SEM-95-001 (available at URL http://www.cec.org/); "U.S. Limits on Species Act Do Not Violate NAFTA Side Deal, Panel Rules," *Inside U.S. Trade* (Sept. 29, 1995); "NAFTA Commission Will Not Investigate Claim that U.S. Failing to Enforce ESA," 12 *Int'l Trade Rep. (BNA)* 1604-1605 (Sept. 27, 1995). For discussion of the logging decision, see Cushman, "Court Fight Over Timber Starts Immediately After Law Is Changed," N.Y. Times, Aug. 28, 1995, at A9; "Trade Pact Invoked to Block Logging Law," *id.*, Aug. 30, 1995, at A10; "Green Groups Challenge U.S. Logging Rule Under NAFTA Side Deal," *Inside U.S. Trade* (Sept. 1, 1995); "Environmentalists Seek Investigation of Logging Rider under NAFTA Side Pact," 12 *Int'l Trade Rep. (BNA)* 1482-1483 (Sept. 6, 1995); Submission on Enforcement Matter, SEM-95-002 (available at URL http://www.cec.org/).

[37] *See* Registry of Submission, SEM-96-002 (available at URL http://www.cec.org/).

NACEC has completed one report in response to a petition regarding an environmental incident in Mexico: the mass mortality of migratory waterfowl at the Silva Reservoir in Guanajuato State.[38] During the 1994-1995 winter season, 20,000 to 40,000 waterfowl (e.g., coots, ducks, and grebes) died at the site. Initially the Mexican government attributed the deaths to poisoning by runoff of the pesticide endosulfan from agricultural areas.[39] Not satisfied with this explanation, the National Audubon Society joined two Mexican environmental groups in requesting a NACEC investigation, the first submission made under NAFTA.[40] Management of migratory bird species has long been a major arena of cooperation among Canada, Mexico, and the United States and migratory birds were recognized as a major component of NACEC's work program.[41] Consequently, NACEC ordered the Secretariat to prepare a report.

The NACEC study group found that while the immediate cause of death was botulism, the birds became susceptible to this infection from debilitating exposure to untreated sewage and to high levels of heavy metals from industrial runoff.[42] While the bird mortality was regrettably high, it underlines the danger presented not only to wildlife but also to the human inhabitants living around the reservoir. The report offered a series of options to mitigate pollution within the reservoir's watershed. It suggested the three countries work jointly on the issue and recommended the establishment of an independent monitoring and reporting group, broadly representative of all interested stakeholders, including non-governmental organizations (NGOs). The report highlighted the necessity for substantial reduction of industrial pollution in the watershed with funding for this project to be sought at the international and regional level.

Also in the Mexican arena, NACEC has accepted a submission seeking to halt the construction of a cruise ship dock adjacent to coral reefs at the resort of Cozumel, Mexico.[43] The complaining parties allege that Mexican authorities

---

[38]   *See* CEC Secretariat Report on the Death of Migratory Birds at the Silva Reservoir (1994-1995) (available at URL http://www.cec.org/).

[39]   DePalma, "Deaths of Birds in Mexico Lake Test Trade Pact," N.Y. Times, June 6, 1995, at A4; "Treaty Partners Study Fate of Birds at Polluted Mexican Lake," *id.*, Aug. 1, 1995, at B6.

[40]   Dillon, "Inquiry Finds Sewage Killed 40,000 Birds," N.Y. Times, Sept. 29, 1995, at A4; Nauman, "NAFTA's First Real Test," *Audubon* 96, 98-99 (Sept.-Oct. 1995).

[41]   *See* Secretariat Report, *supra* note 38.

[42]   *See id.*; Dillon, *supra* note 40. Any contaminant that initially kills the birds increases the chances of a botulism outbreak by contributing carcasses which serve as a protein source for the botulinum toxin.

[43]   *See* Submission on Enforcement Matter, SEM-96-001 (available at URL http://www. cec.org./); "Groups File NAFTA Petition over Port Project in Mexico," 13 *Int'l Trade Rep. (BNA)* 103 (Jan. 1, 1996); Preston, "Where Cruise Liners Intrude, Nafta Tests Waters,"

failed to enforce a number of Mexican environmental laws, including the failure of the project to abide by the environmental impact statement process. On a procedural basis, the Mexican government responded that the complaining parties failed to establish standing, failed to specify any damages they had suffered, and failed to exhaust their remedies under Mexican law. The government also disputed many of the factual assertions in the submission. Nevertheless NACEC has instructed the Secretariat to develop a factual record and the case remains pending at this time.[44]

While NACEC has chosen to pursue only a few of the submissions presented to it, one of its mandates is to involve the public in its decision making. In a discussion paper the Commission recognized that although there is a wide variety of ways in which the public may have both formal and informal input into the decision-making process, the actual entry points for public involvement may not be clear to an outsider unfamiliar with the process.[45] From its own perspective, NACEC identified the problems discussed below as hampering its obligation to promote citizen participation and transparency of process.

Many of the problems have to do with the time, place, and manner of the submission process. For an individual or NGO it may not be clear where the party can exercise most effectively its influence or support of decisions. It may be difficult to discern the most appropriate time in the decision process to approach the Commission or in what capacity. Each member country has a different approach to channeling public involvement with national decision making which impinges on the Commission. There is also the issue of the cost (in financial and human terms) of becoming involved with NACEC decision making. How can NGOs, often with restricted budgets and a host of interests competing for attention, most efficiently partition their resources? How can the Commission facilitate access for those who have only limited financial resources? A related factor is access to technical advice from experts, individuals, and institutions. Currently there is no standard process for deciding how the Commission should ensure adequate geographical, cultural, and sectoral representation. This "inclusionary" process is particularly challenged by the vast cultural diversity among the three member states, a situation which only will grow more complex as new members are added to the NAFTA framework.

The Commission is at such an early stage of its development that it has yet to

N.Y. Times, Feb. 26, 1996, at A5.
[44] *See* Submission, *supra* note 43.
[45] *See* Commission on Environmental Cooperation, Defining Public Participation in the Activities of the CEC (available at URL http://www.cec.org/).

develop a range of effective approaches for ensuring public participation. To assist with the dissemination of its work, NACEC has established a web site [46] to augment its newsletter and has secured a modest amount of funding to support the creation of local projects by NGOs which promote the goals and objectives of the Council's annual work program. At this stage in its development, NACEC has not become what David Wirth warned about in his chapter: a forum to which NAFTA parties remove disputes in an attempt to attenuate or eliminate entirely public participation. Instead the Commission appears to be making a good faith effort to address transparency and public participation issues in a far more inclusive and sophisticated manner than other international trade bodies.[47]

5. ACCESSION

Although early 1995 brought great hopes for progress toward expanding NAFTA membership, momentum waned quickly. The Clinton Administration faced several major impediments. First was whether the no-amendment, fast-track negotiating authority granted by Congress for the NAFTA negotiations would be extended to subsequent accords negotiated with new entrants, particu-

---

[46]   *See* http://www.cec.org/. All materials are available in French, Spanish, or English.
[47]   "NAFTA Partners to Protect Sub-federal Measures from NAFTA Challenges," *Inside U.S. Trade* (Apr. 5, 1996)(bars any existing state and provincial measures -- other than financial services and investment -- from challenge under NAFTA's dispute settlement provisions). Compare the challenge filed by the Ethyl Corp. under the investment provisions attacking Canada's decision to ban importation of a fuel additive ostensibly on environmental grounds. The same additive is manufactured in Canada also for use in gasoline and several provinces permit its use within their boundaries. Ethyl charged that the Canadian action was an attempt to disguise its anticompetitive intent as environmentally motivated. *See* "Proposed Canadian Ban of Gas Additive Violates NAFTA, Says U.S.-Based Ethyl Corp.," 13 *Int'l Trade Rep. (BNA)* 1409-1410 (Sept. 11, 1996); "U.S. Firm to File First-ever Chapter 11 Complaint Against Canada," *Inside U.S.Trade* (Sept. 20, 1996). For a commentary on state and provincial efforts to protect their laws, see Orbuch, "The Impacts of Trade Agreements on State and Provincial Laws," 5 *Clearinghouse on State International Policies* 3 (Dec. 1995).
   In addition to pending decisions described in the text, see Submission on Enforcement Matter, SEM-96-003 (failure of Canadian government to apply, comply with, and enforce habitat protections under Canadian law) and SEM-96-004 (failure of U.S. government to comply with National Environmental Policy Act at Fort Huachuca, Arizona)(both citations available at URL http://www.cec.org/).
   NAFTA's side agreement, despite its lack of enforcement powers, nevertheless may serve to heighten awareness of environmental impacts in other member states, particularly through coverage in the media. *See, e.g.*, "After Death Tied to Pollution, A Warning on the Rio Grande," N.Y. Times, Aug. 14, 1994, at 14; Sherman, "The Friends of the Whales Fight a Salt Factory," *id.*, Apr. 27, 1995, at A4.

larly the front-runner Chile.[48] Congressional Republicans pressed for a fast-track bill that excluded the side agreements from its coverage.[49] Yet the 104th Congress failed to resolve the fast-track issue one way or the other. By the close of 1996, however, Republican members of Congress predicted renewal of the fast-track negotiating authority, including the side agreements, early in the 105th session to avoid the United States being forced to the sidelines while other Latin American countries proceed on their own to negotiate bilateral pacts with Chile and the European Union.[50]

A second issue impeding Chile's accession to NAFTA was whether the labor and environment side agreements to NAFTA would be extended to cover new entrants. At the formal launch of accession talks in June 1995, Chile's representative announced his country would be prepared to sign the agreements immediately, with no modifications.[51] However, labor groups, particularly the AFL-CIO, announced that not only would they oppose extending the existing labor accord to Chile, they also wanted negotiations reopened to amend the existing tripartite agreement.[52] The AFL-CIO proposed to include within the main NAFTA text guarantees of workers' freedom of association, the right to organize, and the rights to bargain collectively in addition to making labor provisions subject to the same dispute settlement rules as trade provisions. Canada soundly rejected any reopening or re-balancing of rights and responsibilities as between current NAFTA members in accession negotiations.[53]

The third problem was a combination of the first two: whether fast-track negotiating authority would be extended to encompass the side agreements as well. A fourth problem concerned Chile's allegedly poor intellectual property

---

[48] *See* "Chile's NAFTA Accession May Slip Next Year If No U.S. Implementing Law," 12 *Int'l Trade Rep. (BNA)* 1609 (Sept. 27, 1995).

[49] Many view labor and environmental concerns as social issues having no place in a trade accord. *See, e.g.*, "MERCOSUR Prepared to Negotiate with NAFTA on Crucial Elements," 12 *Int'l Trade Rep. (BNA)* 2058-2059 (Dec. 13, 1995); "Kolbe Predicts Fast-Track with No Labor, Environment Restraints," *Inside U.S. Trade* (Sept. 27, 1996).

[50] For a description of how Latin American and Caribbean countries are moving forward to establish their own trade regimes, see Rohter, "Free Trade Goes South With or Without U.S.," N.Y. Times, Jan. 6, 1997, at A4.

[51] "Chile Talks May Enter Deep Freeze If Fast Track Slowed, Aninat Says," *Inside U.S. Trade* (June 16, 1995)(quoting Chilean finance minister Eduardo Aninat); "Chile Will Not Complete NAFTA Talks unless Fast-Track Authority is Approved," 12 *Int'l Trade Rep. (BNA)* 1032-1033 (June 14, 1995).

[52] *See supra* note 33; "AFL-CIO to Oppose Chile's NAFTA Entry if Side Accord Not Strengthened," *Inside U.S. Trade* (Apr. 14, 1995).

[53] *See* "Canada Will Resist U.S. Efforts to Reopen NAFTA in Chile Negotiations," 12 *Int'l Trade Rep. (BNA)* 1481-1482 (Sept. 6, 1995).

rights protection. Modernizing its system was proposed as a minimum criterion for entry into negotiations.[54] Whether Chile would be afforded access to binational review panels under Chapter 19 for antidumping and countervailing duty complaints also remained at issue.[55]

Although the formal launch of accession negotiations with Chile began in June 1995, as of this writing only Mexico and Canada have bilateral trade agreements with Chile and neither of those is as extensive as NAFTA.[56] Consequently, while these agreements may facilitate Chile's eventual accession to NAFTA, negotiations on omitted topics must still take place.

For example, the Canada-Chile FTA, signed November 18, 1996 and scheduled to go into effect June 2, 1997, differs from NAFTA.[57] To ensure that trade negotiations proceeded expeditiously, Chile and Canada agreed to omit product standards, intellectual property and sanitary and phytosanitary measures from their bilateral pact, reasoning that their WTO obligations cover those areas sufficiently for the time being.[58] The two parties also excluded government procurement and financial services from the bilateral pact.

In areas that are covered by the agreement, antidumping and rules of origin provisions are more liberal than NAFTA. Instead of providing for dispute resolution under a method like NAFTA's Chapter 19 binational panel approach, the parties agreed to forbid the use of antidumping measures against each other's exports upon the elimination of a tariff or within six years, whichever occurs first. Indeed Canada saw the exclusion of antidumping measures under its bilateral agreement with Chile as setting a precedent for the eventual elimination of antidumping complaints under NAFTA, a proposal which has been greeted very coolly by both the United States and Mexico.[59]

In comparison, the Chile-Canada FTA rules of origin are designed to be transitional rather than permanent. Consequently they are more flexible than those found in NAFTA, primarily because there is no large producer (i.e., the United States) present in the FTA to supply inputs originating within the trade

---

[54] *See* "Cling Peach, Tomato Industry Oppose Chile NAFTA Bid; AT&T Voices Support," 12 *Int'l Trade Rep. (BNA)* 727-728 (Apr. 26, 1995).

[55] *See* "Canada to Use Free-Trade Agreement with Chile to Press U.S. on NAFTA Accession, Chretien Says," 13 *Int'l Trade Rep. (BNA)* 1782-1783 (Nov. 20, 1996).

[56] *See* "Chile-Canada FTA Differs from NAFTA but Could Aid Chile Accession," *Inside U.S. Trade* (Nov. 29, 1996).

[57] *See* "Canada and Chile Reach Free Trade Agreement," 5 *Canada Q.* 4 (Jan. 1997).

[58] *See supra* note 56; Canadian Dept. For. Aff.& Int'l Trade, Canada and Chile Sign Free Trade Agreement, press release 211 (Nov. 18, 1996).

[59] *See* "Canada Seeks Replication in NAFTA of its AD Exclusion with Chile," *Inside U.S. Trade* (Nov. 29, 1996).

area.[60] While these rules of origin are more flexible for manufactured goods (although there are exceptions), rules of origin for agricultural and forest products mirror those of NAFTA. And because this is a bilateral pact, there is no access for third parties to the dispute settlement mechanism. Clearly, major negotiations will be required for Chile to accede to NAFTA in its current form. Extending the agreement to cover all 34 countries in the western hemisphere by the 2005 will be even more problematic.[61]

6. CONCLUSION

This short experience with NAFTA has shown that each party has maintained a distinct identity, yet NAFTA and its side agreements have increased the opportunity for and sensitivity to the need for cooperation across national boundaries. Despite its role as the pre-eminent economic power in the hemisphere, the United States now finds checks on its ability to act unilaterally, as shown by the outcry regarding the Cuban Liberty and Democratic Solidarity Act of 1996, the so-called Helms-Burton law.[62] Similar unilateral foreign policy decisions pro-

---

[60] *See supra* note 56.

[61] Louis Ortmayer's examination of two-level games for the current NAFTA members becomes infinitely more complex for 34 partners. See also the useful working paper series published by the North-South Center at the University of Miami, *Implementing the Summit of the Americas*.

For a fascinating examination of how much labor rights can vary in the western hemisphere, see Comment, "Women Workers in Transition: The Potential Impact of the NAFTA Labor Side Agreements on Women Workers in Argentina and Chile," 17 *Comp. Lab. L.J.* 526-564 (1996). This Comment explores how women traditionally have been encouraged to perform roles primarily as wives and mothers, how they have been excluded or marginalized within the work force as well as within the labor movement itself.

[62] *See* Cuban Liberty and Democratic Solidarity (LIBERTAD) Act of 1996 (Pub. L. 104-114, Mar. 12, 1996, 110 Stat. 785). For reaction to and analysis of the Act, see "U.S. Agrees to Talk with Canada, Mexico on Helms-Burton Sanctions Measure," 13 *Int'l Trade Rep. (BNA)* 476-477 (Mar. 20, 1996); "EU Protests Helms-Burton Law, Asks U.S. To Delay Implementation," *id.* 682-683 (Apr. 24, 1996)(EU protests); "Canada Plans Legislation to Counter Helms-Burton Law," *id.* 1008-1010 (June 19, 1996)(institution of "blocking" orders); "Clinton Delays Lawsuits under Title III of Helms-Burton," *id.* 1158-1159 (July 17, 1996); Ibrahim, "U.S. 3d-Country Sanctions Are Angering the Europeans," N.Y. Times, July 25, 1996, at A4 (includes discussion of sanctions against Libya and Iran); Preston, "Clinton Envoy Finds Mexico Adamant on Cuba," *id.*, Aug. 29, 1996, at A5; Uchitelle, "Who's Punishing Whom?," *id.*, Sept. 11, 1996, at C1, C4; "Canada Introduces Legislation To Counter Helms-Burton Law," 13 *Int'l Trade Rep. (BNA)* 1459 (Sept. 18, 1996); "Mexican Senate Approves Law Countering Helms-Burton Measure," *id.* 1496 (Sept. 25, 1996)(unanimous approval for law offsetting monetary sanctions imposed by U.S.); "Canadian Parliamentarians Criticize Anti-Helms Burton As Ineffective," *id.* 1496-

voked consternation in the past but not to the level seen this time, especially among states in the western hemisphere. Additionally, the global presence of U.S. firms in the post-Cold War world mean such extraterritorial exertions of U.S. policy will be tolerated even less than they were in the past. America's historical enthusiasm for unilateralism can no longer stand by itself. With myriad multilateral engagements, the United States will have to improve its capacity for persuasion.[63]

The opportunity for creative dispute resolution established by the labor and environmental side accords may point the way ahead. These processes have increased transparency of governmental decision making, even if they have yet to check all the flaws in the decisions taken. Although the accords always will be inextricably linked with politics, they nevertheless provide leverage for private citizens and NAFTA parties to ensure that environmental, health, and labor considerations are incorporated in all trade decisions.[64] This development represents a major step forward by ensuring that economic instruments incorporate a new global perspective of sustainability, thereby improving the quality of life not only for NAFTA's current members, but also for those yet to come.

1497 (Sept. 25, 1996); "U.S. To Use All Available Means To Defend Helms-Burton, Envoy Says," *id.* 1824 (Nov. 27, 1996); Sanger, "Europe Takes U.S. To Court In Trade Flap," N.Y. Times, Oct. 2, 1996, at A4; "Canada Backs Cuba Suit," *id.*, Oct. 3, 1996, at A4 (Canada joins EU suit as interested third party); Myers, "One Key Element In Anti-Cuba Law Postponed Again," *id.*, Jan. 4, 1997, at 1, 4 (President Clinton announces he will suspend for six months that portion of the law permitting American citizens to sue any foreign company using American property confiscated during the Cuban revolution); "A Frozen Approach to Cuba," *id.*, Jan. 10, 1997, at A14.

[63] "NAFTA Dispute Settlement Flawed by Politics, Canadian Official Says," 12 *Int'l Trade Rep. (BNA)* 1774-1775 (Oct. 25, 1996); "Canadian Report Urges Policy to Counter U.S. Unilateralism," 13 *Int'l Trade Rep. (BNA)* 47 (Jan. 10, 1996); "Range of Barriers Remain to Trade with Canada, Report Says," *id.* 562-563 (Apr. 3, 1996); "Canada and U.S. Finalize Accord on Softwood Lumber," *id.* 556-558 (Apr. 3, 1996)(5-year pact ends dispute spanning 15 years); Sanger, "Talk Multilaterally, Hit Allies With Stick," N.Y. Times, July 21, 1996, at E3; World Trade Org., Trade Pol'y Rev. Body, Review of the United States; doc. no. iwp960137 (Nov. 12, 1996)(chastising U.S. for "resort to unilateral approaches"). For an examination of previous clashes between the United States and Canada over Cuba policy, see Dallmeyer, "Foreign Policy and Export Controls: How Will the Canada-United States Free Trade Agreement Accommodate the Extraterritorial Application of United States Laws to Canadian Exports of Goods and Technology?," 19 *Ga. J. Int'l & Comp. L.* 565-588 (1989).

[64] For an excellent discussion of how NAFTA's side accords have affected trade negotiations both within NAFTA and in the global arena, see Garvey, "Trade Law and Quality of Life -- Dispute Resolution under the NAFTA Side Accords on Labor and the Environment," 89 *Am. J. Int'l L.* 439-453 (1995). *See also* "Side Pact to NAFTA Doesn't Dispel Policy Tensions, Economist Says," 13 *Int'l Trade Rep. (BNA)* 279 (Feb. 21, 1996)(discussing preference still accorded to trade concerns over environmental protection).

LIST OF CONTRIBUTORS

Léon Bendesky is partner and director of ERI, economic consultants. He has been a professor at CIDE, UNAM, and the Universidad de las Américas, as well as an economist at the Center for Latin American Monetary Studies. In addition to serving as an editorialist for La Jornada, a daily national newspaper, Dr. Bendesky is the author of *Financial Liberalization in Spain, Korea, and Chile* and editor of *The Current Role of the Central Bank*.

Dorinda G. Dallmeyer, research director at the Dean Rusk Center for International and Comparative Law, has edited three Rusk Center monographs on U.S.-Canada relations and also has published several scholarly articles on U.S. trade policy and the FTA. She serves on the advisory board of the Canada-U.S. Law Institute at Case Western Reserve University School of Law and is a member of the Council on Foreign Relations.

Alejandro Nadal is Profesor-Investigador at the Center for Economic Studies, El Colegio de México. He also serves as the coordinator for the Science and Technology Program there. He has published a wide array of books and articles in English and Spanish on economic theory as well as on topics ranging from science and technology policy to trade and sustainable development issues. In 1994 he was a scholar-in-residence at the John D. and Catherine T. MacArthur Foundation.

Serena Nanda is Professor and Chair of the Department of Anthropology at John Jay College of Criminal Justice, the City University of New York. Her publications include *Cultural Anthropology* (5th ed., 1990) and she is co-author with Jill Norgren of *American Cultural Pluralism and Law* (2d ed., 1995).

Jill Norgren is Professor of Political Science at The City University of New York where she teaches courses in politics and law at John Jay College of Criminal Justice and the University Graduate Center. She is co-author of *Partial Justice: Federal Indian Law in a Liberal Constitutional System* (1991), and author of the legal history *The Cherokee Cases* (1995). Professor Norgren co-authored *American Cultural Pluralism and Law* which explores some of the hard choices generated by legal cases involving cultural communities in the United States as they confront the values and legal structure of the dominant society.

Louis L. Ortmayer is Professor of Political Science at Davidson College. He has been a Fulbright Fellow in Germany and a Pew Faculty Fellow in International Affairs at Harvard. He teaches in the areas of international politics and international political economy. In 1993 he served as a lecturer for the U.S. Information Agency in Mexico City focussing on the topic of "NAFTA, United States Policy, and the GATT" and was affiliated with Mexican universities and government ministries during his tenure there.

Robert A. Pastor is the Director of the Latin American and Caribbean Program of the Emory University's Carter Center and Professor of Political Science at Emory University. He is the author of ten books and over 200 articles on U.S. foreign policy and Latin America, including his most recent book, *Whirlpool: U.S. Foreign Policy Toward Latin America and the Caribbean*, published by Princeton University Press. He served as Director of Latin American and Caribbean Affairs on the National Security Council from 1977 to 1981. He also advised the Clinton campaign and administration on NAFTA.

Daniel Salée is Associate Professor of Political Science and Vice-Principal of the School of Community and Public Affairs at Concordia University in Montreal, Canada. He is the co-author of *The Shaping of Quebec Politics and Society* (1992) and *The Quebec Democracy: Structures, Processes and Policies* (1993). His current research and scholarly interests focus on identity politics and the politics of difference in Canada and multicultural societies.

David A. Wirth is Associate Professor of Law at Washington and Lee University where he teaches environmental, administrative, public international, and foreign relations law. Prior to joining the faculty, he served as Senior Attorney and Co-Director of the International Program of the Washington, D.C. office of the Natural Resources Defense Council. He also has been Attorney-Adviser for Oceans and International Environmental and Scientific Affairs in the Office of the Legal Adviser of the U.S. Department of State.

INDEX

NAFTA Law and Policy Series

1. F.M. Abbott: *Law and Policy of Regional Integration: The NAFTA and Western Hemispheric Integration in the World Trade Organization System.* 1995   ISBN 0-7923-3295-4
2. S.J. Rubin and D.C. Alexander (eds.): *NAFTA and Investment.* 1995
                                                 ISBN 90-411-0032-6
3. S.J. Rubin and D.C. Alexander (eds.): *NAFTA and the Environment.* 1996
                                                 ISBN 90-411-0033-4
4. D.G. Dallmeyer (ed.): *Joining Together, Standing Apart: National Identities after NAFTA.* 1997   ISBN 90-411-0483-6

KLUWER LAW INTERNATIONAL – THE HAGUE / LONDON / BOSTON